REI Editions

All our ebooks can be read on the following devices:
- Computer
- eReader
- iOS
- Android
- Blackberry
- Window
- Tablet
- Mobile phone

Brown Kittel

The Yakovlev

Yak-1 - Yak-3 - Yak-7 - Yak-9

ISBN: 9782372975377

Publication: February 2025

Brown Kittel

The Yakovlev

Yak-1 - Yak-3 - Yak-7 - Yak-9

REI Editions

Index

Yakovlev

OKB 115 Yakovlev Design Bureau, named after its founder Alexander Sergeevich Yakovlev, was a Soviet aircraft construction engineering bureau, and today is a joint-stock company of the United Aircraft Corporation group.

The name Yakovlev is widely used in the West, but in Russia it is shortened to Yak followed by the name, or model, of the aircraft.

During World War II Yakovlev designed and produced a famous line of fighter aircraft: the company is, in fact, known for its highly successful line of piston-engined fighter aircraft dating back to World War II:

- Yak-1
- Yak-3
- Yak-5
- Yak-7
- Yak-9
- Yak-15

Yakovlev Yak-1

The Yakovlev Yak-1 was a low-wing fighter/bomber designed by OKB 115 under Alexander Sergeevich Yakovlev and developed in the Soviet Union in the early 1940s.
The Yak-1 was the first, and one of the main fighters of the Yak family, which formed the basis for subsequent types and modifications: the Yak-1 was, therefore, the progenitor of the entire Yak fighter family.
By its purpose, the Yak-1 was a single-seat front-line fighter, and by its design it was a cantilever monoplane, i.e. without struts and braces, with a low wing and conventional landing gear that retracted in flight.

I-26, prototype of the Yak-1.

To reduce development time, the Yak-1 was put into mass production before state tests of prototypes, which resulted in a number of significant flaws, which, however, did not change the aircraft's overall high rating.

- With its wooden wings and steel-tube skeleton, the Yak-1 was an agile, maneuverable and, just as importantly, easy-to-maintain and reliable aircraft.

It proved to be the best fighter in service with the VVS, the Soviet Air Force, at the time of Operation Barbarossa (the code name for the invasion of the Soviet Union by Germany, which began on Sunday 22 June 1941, during the Second World War), when it found itself used against the pressing German war action, contributing, in the following twelve months, to stem the advance of the invaders by fighting in an unfavourable strategic situation.

It should be noted that the first serial I-26 was assembled on March 22, 1940, and the remaining 11 aircraft of the first series - until the beginning of June 1940.

Subsequent modifications to the wing design, made in May, involved the redesign of the entire wing layout, starting with the first aircraft, which had already completed its maiden flight on 7 June 1940.

- Early flights highlighted the need to replace the oil cooler, which did not provide the necessary heat transfer, and the landing gear wheels, which heated up during braking, reducing their effectiveness.

Subsequent changes and modifications continued.

By 1 August 1940, the oil system had been replaced seven times, the air system four times, and the armament and engine cowlings twice each.

In August, the AK-30's air compressor was replaced with an AK-50, as the AK-30 did not provide the air pressure needed to retract the landing gear during take-off, and weight compensation was introduced in the wing and elevator, starting with the first aircraft.

- In total, from 1 February to 1 October 1940, 300 changes were made to the I-26 design and 3,950 to the drawings.

Further assembly and production of the vehicles was delayed due to a lack of engines and propellers. By 10 October only five engines were available, and by 10 November 1940 three sets of propellers.
The Yak-1 was the forefather of a family of models that would be produced, during the conflict, in more than 37,000 units.

History

With the increasing obsolescence of their radial-engined fighters such as the Polikarpov I-16 monoplane and the I-153 biplane, Soviet defense officials issued a specification in 1939 for a new generation aircraft, featuring higher overall performance, though not necessarily more armed and agile than its predecessors.

The design bureaus (OKB) presented four models, three of which were approved and put into serial production: overall, the best proved to be the one designed by Aleksandr Sergeevich Yakovlev, who had already designed racing aircraft and gliders. The aircraft was conceived in four different variants:

- The one called "I-26", represented by a "tactical" fighter aircraft to be used at medium-low altitudes.
- A training variant, "I-27".
- A variant for a high-altitude fighter, "I-28".
- One whose main armament consisted of guns, "I-30".

The prototype, designated I-26, proved to be neither the fastest nor the best armed of the lot, but it was more agile and the most balanced of the three that reached production.

As a reward for his achievement, Yakovlev was awarded the Order of Lenin, the highest decoration awarded by the Soviet Union, and received a prize of 100,000 rubles along with an automobile.

Based on the needs of the Air Force to increase aircraft production, by order of the People's Commissar for Aviation Industry of June 24, 1941, Plant No. 292 was tasked with producing not 1,100, but 1,350 Yak-1 aircraft by the end of the year.

The initial difficulties in starting serial production of the new fighters at Plant No. 292 were due to the fact that many innovations and technical solutions were launched into production without being sufficiently perfected.

In July 1944, production of the Yak-1 ceased, but delivery of combat-ready aircraft to units continued until October: in the period from 1939 to 1944, a total of 8,670 Yak-1 fighters were produced.

The modification of the I-26 for the more powerful experimental M-107 engine, 1,300 hp at 5,000 meters, was started by the design bureau on February 29, 1940 and provided for the transfer of the fighter for state tests, by January 1, 1941, with the following flight data:

- Maximum speed: 650 km/h at 7,000 meters.
- Landing speed: 130 km/h.
- Flight range: 600 km, with additional tanks: 1,000 km.
- Tangency: 12,000 meters.
- Time to climb to 8,000 meters: 8 minutes.
- Armament: One 20 mm cannon and two 7.62 mm shKAS machine guns, supplemented by two 12.7 mm machine guns in the wings. Such a gun arrangement would, however, have required substantial changes to the wing

design and a reduction in the volume occupied by fuel, and, consequently, a reduction in the range and flight duration. Therefore, it was decided to replace the two synchronized ShKAS machine guns with two synchronized 12.7 mm Berezin UB machine guns.

All work was completed on August 22, 1940, but the engine was not yet ready, and to achieve the characteristics specified by the decree, the aircraft was equipped with a high-altitude M-105PD engine with an E-100 compressor.

In May 1941, serial production of the air-cooled M-82 engine began with a rated power of 1,540 hp at 2,050 meters and 1,330 hp. at 5,400 meters.

Intended for installation on fighters, it was not used, since the new fighters launched into series production had water-cooled engines: the engines produced were therefore stored and transported to warehouses.

At the outbreak of war, in order to somehow utilize this reserve of engines, on September 11, 1941, AS Yakovlev gave orders to the head of the TsAGI to carry out aerodynamic calculations of various aircraft, including the Yak-1, by October 20 and to evaluate the improvement in flight performance resulting from the installation of the M-82 engine: the calculations were completed ahead of schedule, by September 30, 1941.

The installation of a new engine on the Yak-1 made it possible to provide for:

- Increased top speed by 30 - 35 km/h.
- Increase in altitude by 1,000 meters.
- Improved rate-of-climb characteristics, reducing the time to reach 5,000 meters by 0.8 - 1.2 minutes.
- Reduction of take-off length by approximately 10%.

However, the dry weight of the M-82 engine was 250 kg more than that of the M-105P; once again, the excellent possibilities for improved flight performance conflicted with the limitation of the airborne weight due to the drag of the landing gear wheels.

- Therefore, the answer to the question about the possibility of replacing the M-105P engine on the Yak-1 with the M-82 turned out to be negative.

1942 began under the banner of streamlining the design of the Yak-1, as the ski chassis, the installation of RS-82 missiles and radio antennas "eaten up" the speed and worsened maneuverability.

Therefore, 10 aircraft of the 60th series were designed and delivered, in a lightweight version without ShKAS machine guns and their ammunition, with unsealed fuel tanks and a metal tail unit, increasing the ammunition for the cannon from 120 to 150 rounds.

- However, when the Germans introduced the new Bf 109G equipped with a DB-605A-1 engine, it was decided to produce 20 Yak-1 aircraft of the 96th series, lightened by a further 160 kg.

The ShKAS machine guns with ammunition and mounts, the pneumatic reloading system, the RSI-4 radio station with mast and antenna, the generator and night equipment were removed from them, and in place of the wooden one a 14 kg lighter metal tail was installed.

Thanks to the reduction in the weight of the car and the improvement of its aerodynamics, the maximum speed increased by 23 km/h, up to 592 km/h at an altitude of 3,800 meters, while the time to climb to 5,000 meters decreased to 4.7 minutes.

During the same period, the problems of improving the aerodynamics of the Yak-1 were solved, which made it possible to achieve similar speeds and maneuverability without removing equipment and weapons, something the army had always been extremely reluctant to do, allowing it only as an exceptional and temporary measure.

- Thus the fate of the lightweight version was once again sealed.

Again, already in July 1943, two Yak-1s with improved visibility and aerodynamics, equipped with the M-105PF engine, were specially lightened for the air defense of the city of Saratov: the reduction of the in-flight weight was achieved by removing the armored backrest and armored glass, the neutral gas system, the emergency landing gear release system and the fuel tank protection.

The decision taken by the government in the spring of 1942 to build a fighter-bomber version of the Yak-1 had a negative impact on the issue of saving weight and recovering speed performance.

- For this purpose, the underwing attachments for the RS-82 rocket projectiles were eliminated and replaced by bomb racks, one per wing, capable of carrying bombs with a maximum total weight of 200 kg.

The modification, which affected the performance of the fighter due to the aerodynamic effect of the rack alone, in addition to the increase in weight due to the bombs, was not appreciated by the pilots, but was in any case maintained on all the models built, until the end of series production.

Towards the end of 1941, construction also began on a two-seater, the Yak-7, but the training tasks of this aircraft were soon outweighed by operational needs and, therefore, given the surprising manoeuvrability it demonstrated, its conversion into a true single-seater fighter was undertaken, the Yak-7B, which benefited from the 1,260 hp VK-105PF engine, in place of the original one.

It is not clear whether the transformation into a "fighting" machine was due to necessity or whether the qualities of the vehicle recommended it.

6,300 Yak-7s were produced, bringing the total of first-generation Yaks to approximately 15,000.

They were used on the front line in both single-seater and two-seater models, especially the latter with aerial observation tasks.

- Although the Yak-1 was later superseded by the later Yak-3 and Yak-9, until 1943 they remained very important for low- to medium-altitude fighter missions.

Initially they were instrumental in enabling the VVS to resist the German attack and then, in addition to continuing to fight fiercely, they laid the foundations of a dynasty that according to some sources reached 37,000 descendants, even more numerous than the Bf 109s and perhaps the Ilyushin Il-2s.

Technique

Built with a robust "mixed" structure, consisting of a fuselage made of a steel truss with an aluminum skin and wooden wings, this small fighter benefited from the designer's experience in building racing machines.
The fuselage design was very simple and clean, with linear structures, a rather large tail and a good level of visibility.

- It was a very robust aircraft, simple to build and very easy to maintain, which were very important to the Soviets.

The factories that produced it were moved 1,600 km back, so as not to be occupied by the Germans, but even so production remained high and by the end of the year there were apparently 500 aircraft in service.
In the meantime, some changes were implemented, within the limits of a machine with no growth potential due to the engine adopted and the very heavy structure: after some "field" modifications consisting in sawing the back of various aircraft, it was decided that also in the production line the aircraft would have to be built with the rear part of the fuselage lowered, giving life to the Yak-1M, characterised by a "teardrop" canopy, among the very first examples of this natural evolution compared to fighters with a "hump" fuselage.

- The wing, built of wood, with two beams, was a single block, and had a trapezoidal shape, with rounded ends: inside them there were no weapons, but a wide-track trolley.

Clark YH airfoil with a relative thickness of 15% on the aircraft's symmetry plane and 7% at the wingtips.

The main structural element of the wing was the front spar with a wing nose up to 8 mm thick, glued with 10 mm three-layer plywood: the rear spar was weaker than the front one and was auxiliary.

Both had a box-shaped section: the shelves are made of glued pine strips, the walls are made of plywood with a thickness varying from 10 mm at the root of the wing to 3 mm at the end.

- There were 46 ribs connected to each other by longitudinal stringers and, together with the terminal arches, they formed the whole wing.

The spars consisted of strips and boards with a cross-section of 8x10 mm: behind the front spar, the wing was covered with 3-5 mm thick Bakelite plywood.

The wing had a smooth surface thanks to the use of plywood, which was glued to the wing frame with casein glue and joined to the spars, to which it was further fixed with screws: afterwards, it was covered with canvas and stucco.

A two-section spoiler was attached to the rear longeron via three milled duralumin brackets: the spoilers were of the "fraise" type, with axial compensation to counteract yaw moment, made of duralumin , riveted, covered in fabric and had 100% weight compensation.

- The left aileron was equipped with a ground-adjustable trimmer.

The main part of the fuselage was a welded metal frame, integral with the engine mount, made in the form of a space truss made of SZOKhGSA pipes with a diameter of 20 to 50 mm.

The welded fuselage was strengthened by steel reinforcements placed at the top and bottom of the truss, between the frames.

Frames 1 and 2 delimited the cockpit: to form the canopy, a frame was welded to the upper longerons, while in the same compartment were located four main and four auxiliary attachment units for the wings and fuselage.

The nose of the fuselage was covered by a cowling made up of seven easily removable covers, three upper, two lateral and two lower, made of 1 mm thick duralumin.

- The lids were fixed to a frame made of duralumin profiles, sewn with a leather strap to ensure a watertight seal.

On the Yak-1 from plant No. 301 there are two upper hoods and four side hoods.

The front upper cover was devoid of the heat-resistant edge of the machine gun grooves, and on vehicles of the first and second series, the rear lower cover featured an air intake for the supercharger of the I-26-I type engine.

The first series of aircraft produced by Plant No. 292 were equipped with "gills" in the rear upper cowling to blow air into the engine compartment.

The Yak-1b was equipped with two upper cowlings, and starting with the 106 series, fairings for the engine exhaust pipes were installed on the side cowlings.

- To give the fuselage an aerodynamic shape, fairings were installed at the top and bottom of the truss.

The upper fairing, which was a continuation of the cockpit roof, was covered in Bakelite plywood: using squares, it was glued to the window retainers, which in turn were fixed to the frame tubes with tarpaulin tape on casein glue.
On the sides of the fuselage were four service hatches with 1 mm thick duralumin covers: right and left cockpit covers, water radiator access hatch covers and tail gear inspection hatch covers.

- The first batch of I-26s from Plant No. 301 did not have a hatch to access the water radiator.

The pilot's seat was height-adjustable, both on the ground and in flight, while at the rear, the pilot was protected by a standard 9mm thick armour plate.
The main landing gear is retracted into the wing nose towards the fuselage by folding the struts with pneumatic cylinders: oil-air damping with braking on the return stroke.
A milled duralumin fork, welded from the 49 series onwards, is mounted on the strut bar, with a flange for mounting the wheel brake, secured with tapered bolts.

- The 600x180 mm cantilever wheel axle with air brake is inserted into the half-fork and secured with tapered bolts.

In the retracted position, the main landing gear was held in place by a pneumatically controlled lock, while in the released position, it was held by a lock on the folding support, which prevented it from closing.
To ensure smooth retraction and release, a hydraulic damper was mounted on the lift cylinder.

- The tail wheel was not retractable, but self-steering and equipped with air-oil shock absorbers: before take-off and landing, it was locked in the neutral position by means of a handle in the cockpit.

From the 127 series onwards, an automatic tailwheel lock was installed, which unlocked the tailwheel when the pedals were tilted more than 20°.
Tail wheel dimensions: 255x110 mm.
In winter, the wheeled chassis was replaced by a ski frame: the main skis, measuring 1650x620 mm, had been specially developed by the design office.

- The total weight of the main skis was 123 kg, while the tail ski was 6 kg.

The elevator and ailerons controls were very precise: the manual control levers were made of 8 mm thick duralumin sheet metal and rotated on ball bearings, while the rods, made of steel and duralumin tubes, moved alternately in guides consisting of three ball bearings.
The engine-propeller group consisted of the M-105P engine, later the M-105PA and, finally, the M-105PF, with water cooling and an automatic three-bladed VISh-61P propeller.

- The engine was started by compressed air from a common cylinder (pressure not less than 50 kg/cm2).

The starter valve and the syringe for filling the cylinders, as well as the piping after the fuel pump, were installed on the right console, while the magnetic switch and the starter button were located on the left.

- The fuel pump driven by the engine.

The fuel was contained in four tanks with a total capacity of 408 litres, two of 130 litres and two of 74 litres, positioned in pairs in the wings, and were protected with anti-icing rubber.

The thickness of the protection on the bottom of the tank was 8 mm, on the sides 6 mm and on the top 4 mm.

The common pipeline, by means of a three-way valve, the control lever of which was located on the left panel, allowed petrol to be consumed from all tanks simultaneously, or separately from the left or right group of tanks.

- The space in the tanks, which was freed up by consuming petrol, is filled with neutral gas.

The lubrication system consisted of a 37-liter tank (42-liter on aircraft from Plant No. 301), a filter, an additional oil booster pump, a C-shaped honeycomb radiator and a network of pipes made of duralumin tubes.

The oil cooler was mounted in a tunnel under the front of the engine: the operation of the system was controlled by a pressure gauge and a thermometer, combined in a single three-point indicator.

- In winter, the oil was diluted with gasoline, which was done before turning off the engine, by pouring gasoline into the oil tank or using the dilution valve on newer production aircraft.

The engine cooling system had a capacity of 75 litres, used water and antifreeze, and was installed under the fuselage, behind the wing.

To retain heat in winter, the top of the water radiator was covered with a heat insulator made of waterproof fabric, and in front of the water radiator there was a heat-insulating partition wall made of the same material.

- The operation of the system was controlled by a water thermometer located on the dashboard.

The equipment for high-altitude flights consisted of a KPA-3 (KPA-3bis) oxygen device with a 4-liter cylinder, installed under the pilot's seat.

The first 1,000 Yak-1s were not equipped with radios: the installation of radios became common from spring 1942 and mandatory from August 1942. However, Soviet radios were unreliable and had insufficient range, so they were often removed to reduce weight.

- The radio equipment installed on the aircraft included: an RSI-4 "Malyutka" receiver, an RSI-3 "Orel" transmitter and an RPK-10 "Chayenok" radio compass.

To the French pilots of the Normandie-Niemen the aircraft, in general, seemed extremely "inspired" by the Dewoitine D.520 and, similarly to the latter, had a 12-cylinder V-engine with a 20 mm caliber cannon firing from the propeller hub, but the engine itself was much more powerful than the French one.

- It was truly of the "French" school since it was derived from the Hispano-Suiza 12Y, and incidentally the power it delivered was what the D.520s would have needed.

In the nose there was space for two 7.62 mm ShKAS machine guns: both these and the 20 mm ShVAK cannon were weapons of absolute excellence in terms of rate of fire, lightness and other qualities, although the weight of the shells and the ammunition supply, 130 rounds for the 20 mm cannon and 750 rounds for the 7.62 mm machine guns, were not entirely adequate to fully exploit their overall qualities.

The spent cases and belt links of the 20 mm gun were ejected under the wing, while the spent cartridges and machine gun links were collected in two bags under the cabin floor.

- Instead of two 7.62 mm machine guns, the Yak-1b had a single 12.7 mm Berezin UB machine gun, positioned on the left, above the engine.

Here too, the spent cartridges and belt links were collected: the spent cartridges in a compartment under the cabin floor, while the belt links in a bag under the machine gun.
The ammunition supply for the machine gun was 220 rounds, while for the cannon it was increased to 140 shells.

The cartridge belts were equipped with:

7.62 mm caliber cartridges:
- 50% - armor-piercing incendiary shells: from a distance of 200 meters they penetrated 7-8 mm armor.
- 25% - armor-piercing incendiary tracer rounds: from a distance of 200 meters they penetrated 6 mm armor: the tracer burned for 700 meters.
- 25% - incendiary targeting shells, which ignited gasoline in unprotected tanks.

12.7 mm caliber cartridges:
- 50% - armor-piercing incendiary shells: from a distance of 200 meters they penetrated 20 mm of armor.
- 10% - armor-piercing incendiary tracer rounds: Damage factors were similar to those above; the burning length of the tracers was 1,000 meters.
- 20% - high-explosive armor-piercing incendiary shells: from a distance of 200 meters they penetrated 15 mm of armor.
- 20% - explosive or incendiary-explosive shells: from a distance of 200 meters they formed a jagged hole with a diameter of 200 mm, while the damage area was caused by fragments with a diameter of 400 mm.

20 mm caliber bullets:

- 30% - Incendiary fragmentation shells: created a 250-300 mm jagged hole and set gasoline alight.
- 70% - armor-piercing incendiary shells: from a distance of 400 meters they penetrated 20 mm of armor and set gasoline on fire.

The aiming system consisted of a reflecting collimator, like the foreign designs of the time.

The aiming system also controlled the "secret weapon" of Soviet fighters, the RS-82 unguided rockets: as for weapons, light machine guns were often replaced by a heavy one, allowing for a better volume of fire.

In the end of the production, in the nose were housed two 12.7 mm Berezin UB machine guns with a total capacity of 700 rounds.

The wings were equipped with RS-82 rockets, widely used in the VVS, used for ground attacks, attacks on bombers and to "scare" fighters: they weighed 24 kg, so the effects, if they hit, were guaranteed, but they were rather imprecise and had to be launched at short distances.

- In place of the 6 rockets, attachments for two 50 or 100 kg bombs were later installed, less spectacular but more effective against ground targets.

By June 22, 1941, the aircraft industry had produced 425 Yak-1 aircraft.

It cannot be said that the Yak-1 was free from design flaws.

The main problem was the fuel leakage from the tanks: in fact, due to the vibrations during landings, the bulkhead that prevented the flow of fuel into the tanks during maneuvers, fixed with spot welding, literally tore the fasteners together with the body of the wall.

Weak pedal design, tail wheel tire failure, severe loosening of fuel tank hatch screws, poor fuel gauge readout visibility, and other shortcomings were noted.

- Additionally, as with other aircraft, humidity caused the plywood skin to warp and crack.

Despite this, all units loved this vehicle: it was simple and easy to fly, and easy to maintain. It is no coincidence that the only female fighter aviation regiment (586th IAP) received 24 aircraft of this type in January 1942: in 125 air battles, the regiment's pilots shot down 38 German aircraft.

In the summer of 1942, new German fighters, the Bf 109G and the Fw 190, began to appear on the front.

The new Messerschmitt, equipped with better armor protection and five gun mounts, was more easily used by German pilots for frontal attacks.

Technical Features

Dimensions and weights

- Length: 8.48 meters
- Wingspan: 10.00 meters
- Height: 2.70 meters
- Wing area: 17.15 m ^{2}
- Empty weight: 2,445 kg
- Maximum take-off weight: 2,950 kg

Propulsion

- Engine: one Klimov M-105PA
- Power: 1,050 hp (722 kW)

Performance

- Maximum speed: 472 km/h at sea level, 569 km/h at altitude
- Climb rate: 877 meters per minute
- Autonomy: 650 km
- Tangency: 10,000 meters

Armament

- Machine guns: 2 x ShKAS 7.62 mm caliber. 1,800 rounds per minute underwing and turret version. 1,625 rounds per minute synchronized version. 3,000 rounds per minute Ultra-ShKAS version
- Guns: 1 ShVAK caliber 20 mm.

Klimov M-105 engine

The Klimov M-105 was a liquid-cooled, V-12 aircraft engine developed from the earlier Klimov M-103, and produced in the Soviet Union from 1939.
The M-105 was designed in the late 1930s using the experience gained from previous designs by the OKB led by Vladimir Yakovlevich Klimov: the M-100 and the M-103.

- In particular, the M-105 maintained the dimensions relating to the bore and stroke of the latter.

The main innovations introduced with the M-105 consisted of the mechanical, two-speed supercharger, the double intake valve for each cylinder and the counterbalancing of the crankshaft.
Produced in approximately 129,000 units, Klimov's V12 acquired during the war, based on the system used by the Soviet authorities, which introduced the identification of the designer by indicating his initials, the new designation VK-105.

Versions

- **M-105**

First version, produced from the end of 1939: it equipped some pre-war fighter aircraft and developed a power of 1,100 hp (820 kW).

- **M-105P**

First mass-produced version: it could house an automatic cannon between the cylinder banks. It equipped most of the Soviet fighters built before the war; power: 1,050 hp (780 kW).

- **M-105PA**

Improved version, produced from 1941, with power equal to 1,200 hp (890 kW).

- **M-105PF (VK-105PF)**

Variant built starting from 1942: the modifications introduced allowed a significant increase in the power delivered, at the expense of performance at higher altitudes.
Despite Klimov's fears that the increased power could lead to a reduction in the engine's life cycle, the production of this version was approved at the urging of Yakovlev's top management, who equipped most of their fighters with this engine.
Power output: 1,260 (p940 kW).

- **VK-105PF2 and PF3**

New versions featuring further increases in power output, 1,300 and 1,360 hp respectively, equal to 970 and 1,015 kW.

- **M-105PD**

This version remained at the experimental stage. Specifically designed for use at higher altitudes, it was equipped with a two-speed "E-100" supercharger and developed a power of 1,170 hp (870 kW).

- **M-105R**

Version designed for use on bomber aircraft. Characterized by a decreased reduction ratio, it developed a power of 1,100 hp (820 kW).

- **M-105RA**

Update of the version specifically intended for bombers, also in this case, acting on the reduction ratio: power equal to 1,110 hp (830 kW).

Characteristics

- Engine: Liquid-cooled V12
- Power supply: carburetor, supercharged
- Distribution: OHV, overhead valves, or in English Over Head Valves (OHV), also commonly called "Rod and rocker arms", with 3 valves per cylinder. This type of distribution improves engine performance and reduces oil consumption, as it allows for a higher compression ratio, optimized intake and exhaust phases, given the smaller size and, therefore, better positioning of the ducts: furthermore, the distribution itself requires less maintenance, as the cams are in a cooler environment and, therefore, are subject to less stress.
- Compressor: Mechanically controlled, dual-speed compressor
- Length: 202.7 cm
- Width: 77.7 cm
- Height: 94.5 cm
- Weight: 575 kg
- Displacement: 35.1 L
- Bore: 148 mm
- Stroke: 170mm
- Compression ratio:
  - ❖ 7.78:1 - 1st speed

- ❖ 11:1 - 2nd speed
- Power:
  - ❖ 1,050 hp (782 kW) at 4,000 meters
  - ❖ 1,100 hp (820 kW) during take-off
- Power/Weight Ratio: 1.42 kW/Kg
- Fuel: 90-96 octane gasoline

Use

By the outbreak of the Great Patriotic War, Soviet industry had produced 425 Yak-1s, but on June 22, 1941, the first day of the German invasion, only 92 machines were operational in the Western military districts, and most were destroyed by the Luftwaffe in the very first days of the war.

- Early combat revealed that the Yak-1 was better than the Bf 109E, but inferior to the Bf 109F, its main opponent.

The Russian fighter was slower and inferior in rate of climb at all altitudes: although it could complete a circle at the same speed as the Bf 109, the lack of automatic controls made dogfighting a complicated affair for the Yak-1, requiring considerable concentration from the pilot.

A Bf 109, with its automatic flaps, had a lower stall speed and was more stable in tight turns and in aerobatic figures in the vertical plane.

Its armament was too light but to reduce weight, modifications were made both on front-line aircraft and on about thirty production machines: the 7.62 mm ShKAS machine guns were removed, leaving only the single 20 mm ShVAK cannon.

These lightened aircraft were much appreciated by the more experienced pilots, for whom a reduction in armament was acceptable: the fighting in November 1942 revealed, in fact, a much more favourable loss/victory ratio.

Furthermore, in the autumn of 1942, the Yak-1B appeared, equipped with the more powerful M-105P engine and a single 12.7 mm UBS machine gun, instead of the two ShKAS: although the use of a single heavy machine gun did not greatly increase the volume of fire, the Berezin UBS proved more effective than the pair of rifle-caliber machine guns.

- Furthermore, on the Yak-1 the PBP collimator was removed, due to the poor quality of the optics, and replaced with the previous, simpler, VV ring model.

Thus modified, the Yak-1 proved very popular with pilots: for Soviet pilot Nikolai G. Golodnikov, overall, considering its tactical and technical characteristics, the Yak-1B was on the level of the Messerschmitt Bf 109G.

The French volunteer pilots of the famous Groupe Normandie-Niémen of Free France, when it was formed in March 1943, selected the Yak-1, in the -1M version, with a "teardrop" canopy and lowered rear fuselage.

The French unit had its first engagement on 5 April 1943, flying from Poltriani-Zavod, southwest of Moscow. But the French suffered their first losses just eight days later, when three Yak-1s were shot down in a skirmish with Focke-Wulf Fw 190s, three of which were claimed.

- Great victories alternated with bitter defeats.

On 22 September, eleven "French" Yaks surprised a Gruppe of Junkers Ju-87 Stukas unescorted by fighters and shot down nine of them without losses: however, during the air battle of Smolensk, nine French pilots were killed and two seriously wounded.

During the first Russian campaign, the Normandie-Niémen lost 23 pilots and claimed 72 kills.

- The Yak-1 was also the aircraft of Lydia Litvyak, the most famous female fighter pilot of all time.

Litvyak flew a "basic" version of the Yak-1, complete with antenna mast, identified by the number "yellow 44".

She served in the 296.IAP unit which later became the 73.Gv.IAP, in May 1943 : Litvyak was shot down and killed in combat on 1 August 1943 at the age of 22, after at least 11 individual and three group victories.

The winter camouflage of Russian fighters was practically white: retractable skis were often mounted, which, however, limited flight performance.

This, together with other production problems, meant that the performance of Russian fighters was often lower than declared, despite the small difference between empty and loaded weight.

German fighters were virtually grounded in winter, not having skis in place of landing gear.

The importance of this model in World War II is often underestimated.

Soviet aircraft naming conventions hide the fact that the Yak-1 and its successors the Yak-3, Yak-7 and Yak-9 were essentially the same model, as with the numerous versions of the Supermarine Spitfire or the Messerschmitt Bf 109.

- And if the Yaks were considered a single model, the 37,000 aircraft produced would make them the largest fighter aircraft built in history.

Losses were proportionally the highest among all fighter models employed by the Soviet Union, both domestic and foreign.

Between 1941 and 1945 they amounted to 3,336 aircraft, of which:

- 325 in 1941
- 1,301 in 1942
- 1,056 in 1943
- 575 in 1944
- 79 in the first four months of 1945.

Yakovlev Yak-3

The Yakovlev Yak-3 was a low-wing multirole fighter designed by OKB 115 under Alexander Sergeevich Yakovlev and developed in the Soviet Union in the 1940s and used primarily by the VVS, the Soviet Union Air Force, in the final stages of World War II.

- Derived from the previous Yak-1, it was robust and easy to maintain, appreciated by both specialists and pilots who appreciated it for its excellent performance in air combat.

It was one of the smallest and lightest fighter aircraft used during the conflict between all belligerents and its high power-to-weight ratio allowed it excellent performance.

According to author Paolo Matricardi, at altitudes between 2,500 and 3,500 meters, the Yak-3 was clearly superior to the British Supermarine Spitfire and the German Messerschmitt Bf 109G and Focke-Wulf Fw 190A.

According to the French ace of World War II with the most kills, 23 aerial victories, Marcel Albert, of the famous Normandie-Niémen Group, who flew both, the Yak-3 was even superior to the North American P-51D Mustang.

- The Yak-3 was the most successful version of the Yakovlev series of fighters, of which more than 34,000 rolled off the factory line during the Great Patriotic War (World War II).

Developed by Antonov, then a member of Alexander Yakovlev's bureau, from the Yak-1M, this aircraft was specifically intended for combat against low- and medium-altitude fighters.

At 2,500 to 3,000 metres, it had superior manoeuvrability and speed to German and Allied aircraft of the time, despite a much lower mass, which earned it the nickname "Mosquito".
The structure had been lightened to the maximum and the engine had been optimised to deliver maximum power below 5,000 metres.

- Towards the end of the war, some examples were fitted with 1,700 hp Klimov Vk107 engines and, later, Vk108.

The Yak-3 was produced in several different versions: 50 metal examples were fitted with new 1,650 hp Klimov VK-107-A engines and armed with two 20 mm cannons. Although it had quite respectable performance, 720 km/h, this version was not mass-produced because Russian officials preferred to keep the Vk-107-A for the Yak-9.
Two further versions were tested, one with a 1,850 hp Klimov Kv-108 engine, equipped with a 23 mm Nudelman-Suranov NS-23 cannon and another with two 20 mm Berezin B-20 cannon.

- Two versions that will be abandoned due to engine overheating.

The most unique feature of the Yak-3 was the fact that it was actually a kind of "disposable" fighter.
It was never designed to last, for example, its wooden parts were not even covered with protective varnish, which explains why 4,848 of them were built in one year.
The Yak-3 had many different versions.

For example, 48 all-metal examples were fitted with a new 1,650 hp Klimov Vk-107A engine and armed with two 20 mm cannons: despite its excellent performance, the aircraft was capable of reaching 720 km/h at 5,750 metres, but was not mass-produced, as Russian leaders preferred to retain the Vk-107A for the Yak-9.

Further tests involved fitting a 1,850 hp Klimov Kv-108 to a Yak equipped with a 23 mm Nudelman-Suranov NS-23 cannon and another equipped with two 20 mm Berezin B-20s. In both cases the engine tended to overheat, ending the project.

- There were also the Yak-3K, designed for anti-tank combat, and equipped with a 45 mm Nudelman-Suranov NS-45 projectile.

Very few examples were built because, once again, the Yak-9 proved to be a better carrier for this weapon.

The Yak-3P was armed with three 20 mm cannons, 596 of which were produced from April 1945 to mid-1946: the Yak-3PD was intended to be a high-altitude interceptor and equipped with a 23 mm Nudelman-Suranov NS-23, but the unreliability of the Klimov VK-105PD left the program without further development.

- Another interesting study was the Yak-3RD, which was a Yak-3D airframe with the addition of a Glushko RD-1 carrier rocket in the tail of the aircraft.

The aircraft demonstrated good performance, 782 km/h at 7,800 meters, but the fatal accident of 16 August 1945 put an end to this project of a fighter with a mixed engine.

The Yak-3T was also supposed to be a tank destroyer armed with a 37 mm gun and two 20 mm guns: this heavy armament resulted in an increase in weight that the engine could not support and, once again, the aircraft was not mass-produced.

The Yak-3U, with its 1,850 hp Shvetsov ASh-82FN engine and two 20 mm Berezin B-20 cannons, was a promising fighter, but its late appearance, well after the end of the war, left it with no hope for the future.

The final variant of the Yak-3 was the Yak-3UTI, featuring a two-seater cockpit and a Shvetov ASh-21 piston engine: it became the prototype of the Yak-11, which had a long and successful career.

The only surviving example of the Yak-3 is on display at the Musée de l'air et de l'espace at Paris-Le Bourget Airport.

The aircraft is presented in the livery of the Normandie-Niémen squadron, composed of French volunteer pilots who decided to fight against the Axis Powers and part of the Soviet VVS.

The only surviving Yak-3 on display at Le Bourget.

History

In 1941 Yakovlev began studying a radical improvement of the design of his first fighter, which had just entered the line.

His efforts were embodied in this small aircraft, equipped with the most essential structure possible around the most powerful engine available, which was still the VK-105PF of the Yak-1M.

- The production Yak-3 was very similar to its predecessor: it retained the cantilevered monoplane structure and three-bladed propeller for an inline engine.

However, it differed from the previous model in that the large oil radiator under the nose had been replaced by a pair of smaller radiators, recessed into the wing roots, which in turn were smaller than the Yak-1, reducing aerodynamic drag.

The rear part of the fuselage, of mixed metal and wood construction, protected by a thick layer of long-lasting wax, was also lowered, allowing, thanks also to the adoption of a "drop-shaped canopy", better visibility.

The result was a fighter that performed better in dogfights than the Yak-1 and Yak-9, although it landed at a higher speed.

- Furthermore, at low altitude, the speed was at least 50 km/h higher than that of other Yakovlevs, as well as the best German aircraft.

The weight of the Yak-3 was so low that it was comparable only to that of the Japanese Zero, even though the ammunition load was limited to 120 20 mm and 500 12.7 mm rounds.

Among the most interesting features of the project was the feature that the driver had a glass shield behind him so as not to be impeded in his rearward vision, even if there was no rear-view mirror to facilitate this.

Developments of this project, one of the most agile fighters of the Second World War, included the powerful Yak-3 re-engined with the 1,650 hp VK-107, capable of 720 km/h and a rate of climb of 1,600 meters per minute, against the 1,300 of the previous one, which however proved less suitable than the Yak-9 to house the more powerful engine.

Yakovlev Yak-3M.

Other interesting developments were experimental aircraft with a liquid-fuel rocket engine in the tail, for a maximum speed of 780 km/h, or with two ramjets under the wings, an aircraft designated Yak-7RD.

The important two-seat trainer Yak-11, with a 700 hp radial engine, metal wing and limited combat capabilities, was also derived from the Yak-3.

Even what can be considered the first of the Soviet jet fighters, the Yak-15, was derived from the Yak-3 but with a 900 kg thrust engine in the nose, and the exhaust in a ventral position, thanks to a steel protection structure.

It was not a great success, especially due to its very modest autonomy but also due to its limited speed of 780 km/h: however, it served to gain experience with the numerous subsequent post-war Yakovlevs with jet engines, starting with the Yak-17, slightly improved compared to its predecessor, with greater autonomy, but with a speed reduced by a few dozen km/h.

Technical Features

Dimensions and weights

- Length: 8.49 meters
- Wingspan: 9.20 meters
- Height: 2.42 meters
- Wing area: 14.83 m ^{2}
- Wing loading: 179 Kg/m ^{2}
- Empty weight: 2,250 kg
- Maximum take-off weight: 2,660 kg
- Built: 4,848

Propulsion

- Engine: a 12-cylinder VKlimov VK-105PF-2
- Power: 1,300 hp (956 kW)

Performance

- Maximum speed: 655 km/h at 3,100 meters
- Climb rate: 18.5 meters per second
- Autonomy: 900 km
- Tangency: 10,700 meters

Armament

- Machine guns: 2 x Berezin UB 12.7 mm caliber with a rate of fire of 800-1,050 rounds per minute
- Guns: 1 x 20 mm ShVAK in the propeller hub
- Missiles: 6 RS-82 rockets.

Use

The Yak-3 was highly appreciated by pilots and ground personnel.

It was robust, easy to maintain and, above all, a highly effective air superiority fighter, although among the unsolved wartime problems was the tendency of the plywood surfaces to peel off when the aircraft was pulled out of a high-speed dive.

It was used mainly as a tactical fighter, flying over battlefields and engaging in combat with German fighters below 4,000 metres.

- In the hands of a good pilot, the Yak-3 could successfully compete with the best enemy aircraft.

The armament of one 20 mm cannon and two 12.7 mm machine guns was virtually identical in both composition and positioning (engine gun with muzzle in the propeller hub and machine guns in the engine cowling synchronized with the propeller) to that of the latest versions of its main contemporary opponent, the Messerschmitt Bf 109G.

This aircraft began to arrive at the Soviet front-line units in the summer of 1944. Operational tests were conducted by the 91.IAP of the Second Air Army, commanded by Lieutenant Colonel Kovalyov, in June-July 1944.

This regiment was entrusted with the task of ensuring air superiority: during the 431 missions carried out, the unit shot down 20 Luftwaffe fighters and three Ju 87s, while Soviet losses were two destroyed Yak-3s.

On June 16, 1944, a major air battle broke out when 18 Yak-3s clashed with 24 German fighters: the Soviet pilots shot down 15 Luftwaffe aircraft for the loss of one Yak shot down and one damaged.

The following day, Luftwaffe activity in that area was virtually suspended: after clashes with this aircraft during the Battle of Kursk in the summer of 1943, the Luftwaffe recognized that the Yak-3 was a powerful opponent.

As proof of this, on 14 July 1944, a formation of 18 Yak-3s clashed with 30 Luftwaffe fighters, shooting down 15 for the loss of only one Yak: and three days later, eight Yaks attacked a formation of 60 German aircraft, including the escort.

- In the ensuing fierce fighting, the Luftwaffe lost three Junkers Ju 87s and four Bf 109Gs, while the Soviets suffered no losses.

That same year, a general directive sent to German units on the Eastern Front recommended "not to engage in combat at altitudes below 5,000 meters with Yakovlev fighters without an oil cooler under the nose and with an inclined antenna mast."

In fact, most Yak-3s had no such mast at all, and the antenna wire was simply stretched between the cockpit and the rudder.

By the end of the war, many front-line units were equipped with this agile fighter, despite its reduced payload and range. Among these was the Normandie-Niemen Group, made up of French volunteers, who, given the choice between American, English and Russian fighters, switched from the Yak-9 to the Yak-3, achieving its last 99 victories of the war, out of 273, on this fighter.

Technique

The production Yak-3 was externally very similar to the Yak-1, retaining its monoplane structure with the wing connected to the lower section of the low fuselage and the teardrop canopy already employed on the Yak-1B version.

However, it differed from the previous model in that the large oil radiator under the nose had been replaced by a pair of smaller radiators, recessed into the wing roots, which in turn were reduced in surface area and span compared to those of the Yak-1, in order to reduce their weight and aerodynamic resistance.

Yak-3.

The weight of the Yak-3 was reduced by almost 200 kg compared to the Yak-1.

From a structural point of view, the Yak-3 presented, instead, important innovations both in the wings, in which the spars and part of the ribs were made of duralumin, and in the covering, for which plywood was used, initially only in the wings, later also in the rear area of the fuselage.

The landing gear, a constant critical element in the Yak-1, was modified in design and strengthened in structure but once again, during use, cases of fragility were encountered which led to the collapse of the legs or the breakage of the attachment points inside the wing.

- The fighter's design was simple and rational.

The fuselage was based on a tubular steel truss: to reduce weight, the fuselage frame was made integral with the engine mount.

The forward section of the fuselage was covered with easily removable duralumin cowlings, while the tail section was covered with plywood: the Yak-3's wing was made in a single piece with two spars.

The airfoil was the "Yakovlev standard" Clark YH, with a relative thickness of 14% at the root and 7% at the wingtip.

The wing had a metal structure with spars, ribs and plywood skin: as on the Yak-9, the skin was glued to special plywood layers riveted to the metal frame.

- After the war, a wing with duralumin skin was developed for the Yak-3, but this aircraft was not mass-produced.

The fighter's powerplant consisted of a VK-105PF2 engine with a capacity of 1,240 hp (935 kW) with a VISh-105SV-01 automatic variable-pitch propeller.

The last series of aircraft built, identified as Yak-3/VK-107A, installed the newer Klimov VK-107: this engine, although less reliable, with its 1,500 hp (1,119 kW) was able to guarantee a significant increase in the aircraft's speed performance.

- The fuel tanks, as on all Yakovlev fighters, were located in the wing and their total volume was 370 liters.

The water radiator was installed behind the cockpit: the peculiarity of the installation of the water radiator on the Yak-3 was that it was deeply "recessed" into the fuselage, and the air supply channel to the radiator was significantly enlarged.

This resulted in a decrease in the speed of the air flow over the radiator itself: as a result, the cooling efficiency was increased and the aerodynamic drag of the radiator itself, as well as of its external fairing, was significantly reduced.

The same principle was used in the design of oil coolers.

- The Yak-3's armament consisted of a ShVAK motorized cannon and two synchronized Berezin UB machine guns.

To make the Yak-3 as light as possible, it was equipped with the minimum necessary on-board equipment, which allowed it to fight during the day in normal weather conditions.

One of the few mandatory equipment was a radio that provided two-way radio communications.

The release and retraction of the landing gear, landing flaps and brake control on all Yakovlev fighters were carried out by a pneumatic system.

Compared to the hydraulic systems used for these purposes on Lavochkin fighters or the electrical systems of American fighters, pneumatic systems were less reliable and caused many problems for mechanics, but the weight savings amounted to tens of kg.

Versions

- **Yak-3**

The main version.

- **Yak-3 (VK-107A)**

Version equipped with a 1,650 hp (1,230 kW) Klimov VK-107A engine and armed with two 20 mm Berezin B-20 cannons with 120 rounds. After several mixed-technique prototypes, serial production of 48 all-metal units was started in 1945–1946. Despite its excellent performance, at 720 km/h at 5,750 meters the VK-107 engine was subject to overheating and it was decided to give priority to its supply to the Yak-9.

- **Yak-3 (VK-108)**

Yak-3 (VK-107A) modified with the 1,850 hp (1,380 kW) VK-108 engine, armed with a single 23 mm Nudelman-Suranov NS-23 aircraft cannon with a firing range of 60 rounds.
During test flights the aircraft reached a speed of 745 km/h at an altitude of 6,290 metres but suffered from an undesirable tendency to overheat.
Another Yak-3 equipped with two Berezin B-20s was fitted with the same engine but with similar results.

- **Yak-3K**

version equipped with a 45 mm Nudelman-Suranov NS-45 gun, built in small series as the Yak-9K, similar in role, was more suitable for the weapon.

- **Yak-3P**

Version produced from April 1945 until mid-1946, armed with three 320 mm Berezin B-20 guns, with 120 rounds for the central gun and 130 for the side guns.

  - The total weight of the guns and shells of the three-gun configuration was, in fact, 11 kg less than that of the armament and ammunition of a standard Yak-3.

The mass fired in one second of fire was 3.52 kg, a value higher than that of most contemporary fighters.

From August 1945, all Yak-3s were in the Yak-3P configuration, with a total of 596 built.

- **Yak-3PD**

High-altitude interceptor fighter version powered by a Klimov VK-105PD and armed with a single Nudelman-Suranov NS-23 with 60 rounds.

Although it reached an altitude of 13,300 metres in flight tests, it did not enter production due to the poor reliability of its engine.

- **Yak-3RD (Yak-3D)**

Experimental version equipped with an additional Glushko RD-1 liquid-fueled rocket engine with 2.9 kN thrust, installed in the modified tail, armed with a single Nudelman-Suranov NS-23 with 60 rounds.

On May 11, 1945, the aircraft reached 782 km/h at 7,800 meters.

During a flight on the following August 16, the aircraft crashed for unknown reasons, killing test pilot VL Rastorguev.

Like all mixed-propulsion aircraft of the period, the project was abandoned in favor of turbojet engines.

- **Yak-3T**

Anti-tank version equipped with one 37 mm Nudelman N-37 cannon with 25 rounds and two Berezin B-20 cannons with 100 rounds.
The cockpit was moved back 40 centimetres to compensate for the heavier nose.
Engine modifications required to incorporate the weapons led to serious overheating problems which were never resolved and the aircraft never progressed beyond the prototype stage.

- **Yak-3T-57**

A single Yak-3T equipped with a 57 mm OKB-16-57 cannon.

- **Yak-3TK**

Version Equipped with a VK-107A engine equipped with a turbocharger powered by exhaust gases.

- **Yak-3U**

Yak-3 powered by a 1,850 hp (1,380 kW) Shvetsov ASh-82FN radial in an attempt to increase performance while avoiding the overheating problems of the VK-107 and VK-108.
The wingspan was increased by 20 cm, the wings moved forward by 22 cm, the cockpit raised by 8 cm and it was armed with two 20 mm Berezin B-20 cannons with a capacity of 120 rounds.

Yak-3U.

The prototype reached a speed of 682 km/h at 6,000 metres, but, although it was considered a success, it was not sent to series production because it was completed after the end of the conflict.

- **Yak-3UTI**

Two-seat trainer conversion based on the Yak-3U equipped with a Shvetsov ASh-21 radial engine.
The aircraft later became the prototype of the Yak-11.

Yak-11

The Yakovlev Yak-11 was a single-engine low-wing trainer designed by OKB 115 under Alexander Sergeevich Yakovlev and developed in the Soviet Union from the mid-1940s.
Used in subsequent years mainly by the VVS, it remained operational from 1947 to 1962 in national flight schools and pro-Soviet air forces.

- Based largely on the design of the excellent Yak-3 fighter used so successfully by the Soviets during World War II, the Yak-11 became the most widely used trainer aircraft by the Soviet Air Force, rivalling in importance the American North American T-6 Texan in its role.

The first prototype flew for the first time on 10 November 1945 and entered service in 1946.
A total of 3,859 aircraft were produced between 1947 and 1956, with another 707 produced under license by the Czechoslovakian Let Kunovice under the designation Let C-11.
Both the Yak-11 and the C-11 were used in flight schools in all Warsaw Pact countries, as well as in many African, Middle Eastern and Asian countries such as Afghanistan, Albania, Algeria, Austria, Bulgaria, China, Czechoslovakia, North Korea, Egypt, East Germany, Indonesia, Iraq, Poland, Romania, Syria, Somalia, Hungary, Soviet Union, Vietnam, Yemen.

- In 1958, a new version, the Yak-11U, was introduced, which was intended to replace it in the training of new Soviet fighter pilots.

The development of the Yak-11U was mainly based on the adoption of a front tricycle landing gear, instead of the traditional one, designed to train pilots in take-off and landing maneuvers with a landing gear now used by all Soviet jet aircraft: produced in limited numbers, however, it did not replace, as planned, its predecessor which managed to remain operational in the VVS until 1962.

Thanks to its notable similarity to the fighter from which it was derived (the Yak-3), the Yak-11 has achieved considerable success among lovers of warbirds, the historic military aircraft that groups of enthusiasts and organizations dedicated to the recovery and preservation of historic aircraft conserve and restore to flying condition to use in air shows.

- Furthermore, thanks to its agility and speed for its class, it is also used in air competitions: currently there are approximately 120 Yak-11s in flight conditions distributed throughout the world.

The Yak-11 retained many features of its predecessor.
The fuselage was made of mixed technique, with a metal structure covered with plywood panels and integrated a tandem two-seater cockpit closed by a long canopy.

The rear ended in a traditional, single-fin tail fin.

The wing was low and cantilevered and incorporated a traditional tricycle landing gear, retractable inward at the front and complemented by a rear jockey wheel.

- Propulsion was provided by a Shvetsov ASh-21 radial engine producing 580 hp (427 kW) coupled to a two-bladed fixed-pitch propeller and enclosed by a cowling with side vents similar to those used on the Focke-Wulf Fw 190.

This last detail is what makes it visibly recognizable from the Yak-3 from which it derives, equipped, instead, with a more powerful V12 Klimov VK-105PF-2 with liquid cooling.

Technical features

Dimensions and Weights

- Length: 8.20 m
- Wingspan: 9.40 m
- Height: 3.28 m
- Wing area: 15.40 m²
- Empty weight: 1,900 kg
- Max take-off weight: 2,440 kg
- Fuel capacity: 230 kg

Propulsion

- Engine: one Shvetsov ASh-21, 7-cylinder radial, air-cooled
- Power: 580 hp (427 kW)

Performance

- Max speed: 465 km/h
- Autonomy: 1,250 km
- Tangency: 7,950 meters

Armament

- Machine guns: one Berezin UBS caliber 12.7 mm or one ShKAS caliber 7.62 mm
- Bombs: 200 kg mounted on two wing racks

Yakovlev Yak-5

The Yakovlev Yak-5 was a single-seat, single-engine, low-wing monoplane trainer aircraft, designed by OKB 115 under the direction of Alexander Sergeevich Yakovlev.

Derived from the previous two-seater Yakovlev UT-2, and intended to equip the fighter training units of the VVS, during the final stages of the Second World War, it was the first Yakovlev model to introduce the variable pitch propeller.

Although it proved suitable during flight tests, its series production never started due to mistrust towards its structure, still mainly made of wood, in favour of the metal-built Yak-18.

By 1944, the Yakovlev UT-2 was the standard primary trainer with which Soviet Air Force training units were equipped: however, due to its basic features, the model proved to be inadequate in effectively preparing pilots destined for more sophisticated aircraft.

To overcome this problem, OKB 115 began designing a more sophisticated variant, the UT-2L, with a revised structure that integrated a single tandem two-seater cockpit enclosed by a long canopy, and adopted wing flaps and instrument flight equipment.

- At the same time, the OKB developed a single-seater model based on the UT-2L design and intended for fighter training.

The aircraft, designated as the Yak-5, was a low-wing monoplane of all-wooden construction which, unlike the UT-2, had the front cockpit removed and adopted a sliding canopy over the rear cockpit.

The landing gear was also modified, adopting a retractable solution in the wing plane instead of the fixed landing gear of the UT-2.

Propulsion was provided by a Shvetsov M-11D five-cylinder air-cooled radial aircraft engine producing 115 hp (86 kW) and mated to a two-bladed variable-pitch propeller.

- The take-off weight was 940 kg, the maximum speed, with the M-11D engine, reached 250 km/h, while the landing speed was 85 km/h, with a flight range of 450 km.

Yak-5.

The model, equipped with a radio transceiver, could be fitted with a 7.62 mm ShKAS machine gun, chambered for 7.62×54 mm R ammunition, synchronized and firing through the propeller disc .

Thanks to more complete flight and navigation equipment, including a powerful landing light, it became possible to conduct training with the Yak-5 in difficult weather conditions and at night.

The prototype Yak-5 took to the air for the first time on 7 September 1944.

- During the subsequent flight tests, the test pilots who took over at its controls supported the quality of the project, appreciating its handling qualities and the aircraft successfully passed the official evaluation.

However, neither the UT-2L nor the Yak-5 were put into serial production as the Soviet Air Force command believed that wooden aircraft were becoming obsolete, which would have led to the production of the all-metal Yak-18 counterpart in late 1945.

- The only Yak-5 was destroyed in a flight accident when, during the execution of a whip, a structural failure of the wooden wing occurred, causing the aircraft to crash.

A snap roll is an aerobatic maneuver similar to a spin, where the aircraft is rotated without using the ailerons, while still remaining in horizontal flight.

As mentioned, the Yak-5 was not mass-produced: however, taking into account the experience gained in designing, building and operating the Yak-5, in 1945 the design team developed the Yak-11 trainer fighter, equipped with an ASh-21 engine with a power of 570 hp and a maximum speed of 465 km/h.

Yakovlev Yak-7

Its history is very original, as it was originally conceived to give Soviet pilots an adequate aircraft for advanced training: soon, however, the machine proved to be so promising, fast and easy to handle that it was considered a front-line aircraft, surpassing its direct progenitor.

The Yakovlev Yak-7 was, in fact, a low-wing trainer aircraft, later converted into a fighter, designed by OKB 115 directed by Aleksandr Sergeevič Jakovlev and developed in the Soviet Union in the 1940s.

- Derived from the previous Yak-1, it was used mainly by the VVS during the Second World War and, from the end of the conflict, by some pro-Soviet air forces.

Designed as an aircraft for the transport and training of aircrew during the transition to new equipment, the Yak-7 subsequently underwent a series of extraordinary transformations and played a far more important role than it was originally intended for.

No less surprising in their nature and results were all the subsequent transformations of the Yak-7 into a fighter aircraft.

- During its serial production, the Yak-7 underwent 18 major modifications, including: 5 to the airframe, 6 to the engine, 7 to the armament and one to the special equipment.

It should be noted that major modifications of the Yak-7 and other Yak aircraft included those involving the installation of a new engine, new weapons, or significant changes in the design of the airframe, and were usually accompanied by the assignment of some index to the aircraft.

Indeed, modifications such as the installation of new water and oil radiators, a tail wheel, the lowering of the cowling and the giving of a more aerodynamic shape to the fuselage were not considered major modifications.

- Thus, the Yak-7, with the M-105PA engine and VISh-61P propeller, was a modification of the Yak-7UTI two-seat trainer fighter, transformed into a single-seat fighter.

Between 1941 and 1944, 6,399 Yak-7 aircraft were produced in various versions, including 5,120 in the Yak-7B version with the M-105PF engine.

History

The Yak-7 began life as a training aircraft derived from the Yak-1 (originally known as the I-26), in early 1940.

On March 4, 1940, the government decided to create a two-seater, dual-control trainer fighter, designated Yak-7 (UTI-26), by modifying the Yak-1 (I-26).

- Furthermore, the I-26's design facilitated its transformation into a trainer fighter.

The result of this process was the first prototype, designated UTI-26-1, which was essentially an I-26 with a two-seater cockpit and the wing moved 10 cm towards the tail, in order to balance the aircraft's centre of mass.

Armament consisted of two 7.62 mm ShKAS machine guns with 500 rounds of ammunition each.

The prototype flew for the first time on 23 July 1940 and underwent flight tests required by the state authorities between 28 August and 19 September.

Yakovlev was given the job because, among all the leading designers of new fighters, he was the only one who had experience in designing trainer aircraft and could approach the task in the best possible way.

Further modifications and improvements were introduced on the second prototype, the UTI-26-II, which was built together with the first.

The chassis underwent significant changes: first of all, the diameter of the landing gear wheels was increased to 650 mm and that of the tail wheel to 300 mm.

- The next major change was an increase in the area of the stabilizer and rudder: from 1.82 m^2 to 1.93 m^2 and from 1.12 m^2 to 1.23 m^2 respectively.

This helped to significantly improve the aircraft's aerobatic properties and its stability in flight.

At the end of the state tests, which took place from January 1 to February 14, 1941, the UTI-26-II received a much more positive assessment from the employees of the Air Force Research Institute than the I-26 six months earlier.

- In terms of performance, the UTI-26-2, the second prototype, came very close to its predecessor, allowing it to develop a maximum speed of 586 km/h at 4,500 metres.

The space required for take-off was 310 metres, while that for landing was 750 metres, also due to the structural fragility of the landing gear, which discouraged the sudden use of the braking system.

The need to equip flight schools with the new aircraft was so great that, in accordance with the order of the People's Commissariat of Aviation Industry dated March 4, 1941, Moscow Aircraft Plant No. 301 had to stop production of the Yak-1 and start producing training aircraft, which received the designation Yak-7UTI.

- The work was carried out at plant N301 immediately after the outbreak of the war.

The first serial number of the machine 01-02 flew on March 18, 1941: although the prototype of the Yak-7UTI aircraft had the same drawback that constantly plagued Yakovlev's designs, namely engine overheating, in the serial machines this was avoided by reducing the engine speed from 2,700 rpm to 2,350 rpm.

Furthermore, the aircraft design was also simplified due to the abandonment of the right-hand 7.62 mm ShKAS machine gun.

Moscow factories produced Yak-7UTI from April to September 1941, that is, until the evacuation, then production was resumed at Novosibirsk plant number 153.

A total of 186 machines of this modification were produced , after deducting 62 Yak-7 fighters produced, it follows that in 1941 as many as 145 Yak-7UTIs left the factory workshops.

In the assignment for 1941, the construction of 6,000 training machines was established, but the war prevented the implementation of these plans: the front required fighters, and in the production of the Yak-7UTI there was a break that lasted seven months.

Some of the training aircraft, after installing the AFA-1M camera in the rear cockpit, were used as reconnaissance aircraft under the designation Yak-7R, however, it was not officially approved.

Subsequently, a production Yak-7UTI N04-11 was taken and the following modifications were made to it: an armored backrest was installed in the rear cabin, the photographic equipment was removed, and the unsealed tanks were replaced with sealed ones.

- Armament-wise, a 20 mm ShVAK motorized cannon with 120 rounds, two 7.62 mm ShKAS synchronized machine guns with 1,500 rounds and six rocket launchers, three under each wing, for RS-82 rockets were installed.

RS fire control was via the ESBR-3 electric bomb release, located on the left cockpit control panel.

Compared to the Yak-1, the single-seater Yak-7 became more advanced and had the following advantages: the dimensions of the chassis wheels fully corresponded to the flight weight, the engine mount, made detachable, made it possible to modify the aircraft for the installation of a different engine, in addition, due to the forward shift of the center of gravity from 26 to 20-21%

of the maximum acceleration coefficient, longitudinal stability increased significantly.

The second (unequipped) cabin could be used to transfer technical personnel and cargo during unit transfers, to ferry pilots from emergency landing sites, to house an additional fuel tank, photographic equipment, bombs or for other purposes.

These features of the Yak-7 made it promising and allowed for further modifications, the most interesting of which was the new method of attaching the propeller nose cone, copied from the German Bf-109: now its assembly and disassembly had become much simpler.

- It was also proposed to produce the aircraft in an improved version, which would allow, if necessary, to install the M-107 engine.

The single-seat fighter and two-seat trainer versions of the Yak-7 had few design differences and their production was standardized, which was of great importance during the war.

- The Yak-1 and Yak-3 could be distinguished from the Yak-7 and Yak-9 by their appearance.

The presence of a second cabin caused a shift in the aircraft's centre of gravity, so the water radiators were moved forward.
This allowed for quick identification: on the Yak-7 and Yak-9, the leading edge of the radiators was located at the level of the front edge of the cabin, while on the Yak-1 and Yak-3, the leading edge of the radiators was located halfway along its length.
In addition, when the planes were on the ground, there was another sign by which it was easy to distinguish these two lines of fighters: the Yak-1 and Yak-3 had a protection on the main landing gear consisting of two parts, while for the Yak-7 and Yak-9 the protection was single.

Starting from the early months of 1942, some modifications were introduced to the fighter version, the result of which is generically referred to as the Yak-7A version, while another important variant was the Yak-7B with M-105PF engine.

Yak-7A

It featured the following design improvements:

- A transceiver station was installed, starting from the 31st aircraft of the 16th series, which included: an RSI-4 ("Malyutka") receiver, an RSI-Z ("Eagle") transmitter, a radio station control panel, Umformers RUN-30 and RU-11-A and the antenna.
  The receiver was on the right dashboard panel and the transmitter was behind the back of the pilot's seat. The radio station control panel was above the right cockpit control panel.
  The antenna was equipped with a shock absorber to ensure the tightness and integrity of the cable under various aerodynamic loads.
  All units of the radio station were interconnected via shielded cables.

- According to TsAGI recommendations, the aircraft's aerodynamics were improved, with the tailwheel being made partially retractable.
  The movable part of the rear cabin roof was replaced by a plywood panel.

- To reduce the take-off run, engine afterburner control was installed, with forced opening of the supercharger throttle valve, which increased the volume of air entering the engine, thus increasing its power.
  The afterburner control knob was installed on the left panel, on the same axis as the normal gas selector and altitude corrector.

- A new mechanism was installed that operated the wing flaps in only two positions instead of three: 0 and 55°, instead of 0, 15° and 55°.
  In fact, a 15° deviation, which should have been used to shorten the length and time of the take-off run, and to reduce the radius and time of the turn, had proved useless.

- The armament of the Yak-7A did not differ from the armament of the Yak-7 and consisted of a 20 mm ShVAK motorized cannon with 120 rounds of ammunition and two 7.62 mm ShKAS synchronous machine guns with a total of 1,000 rounds. Only some constructive improvements were made in the installation of the weapons.

- As a result of improved aerodynamics, the maximum speed of the Yak-7A, compared to the Yak-7, was increased across the entire altitude range: with a ski landing gear of 10 km/h and with a wheeled landing gear of 20 km/h, with speeds, therefore, up to 495 km/h at sea level and up to 571 km/h at an altitude of 5,000 meters.
  The time to climb to 5,000 meters was 6.52 minutes.

Yak-7B

The Yak-7B was a further development of the serial Yak-7A and differed from it by more powerful armament and aerodynamic improvements.

The armament of the Yak-7B consisted of a 20 mm ShVAK cannon with 120 rounds and two 12.7 mm Berezin UBS synchronous machine guns with a total of 400 rounds: the left machine gun with 260 rounds, the right machine gun with 140 rounds.

- Additionally, six RS-82 missiles or two bombs of 25 to 100 kg each could be suspended under the wing.

The armament was successfully tested on the Yak-7B in June 1942.

25 flights were performed with a total duration of 7 hours and 57 minutes, however, according to the GKO decree of May 10, 1942, the Yak-7B was then produced without RS-82 missiles.

- The tail wheel was made fully retractable.

To increase the engine speed from 2,350 to 2,700 rpm, which was necessary to improve take-off and other characteristics of the aircraft, the adjusting ring was removed from the propeller hub: as a result, the installation angle of the VISH-61P propeller blades was decreased from 23 to 20°.

- The increased weight of the guns, however, led to a shift of the center of gravity forward, so from 20 May 1942, an additional tank with a capacity of 80 liters was installed in the rear cockpit.

The pilots were dissatisfied with the installation of such an unprotected tank, as it increased the flight weight and, consequently, worsened the flight performance of the aircraft, as well as increasing the risk of fire in case of being hit.

During the Battle of Stalingrad, this tank was recognized as unnecessary and was , therefore, removed from the aircraft without any instructions from above: officially, this was sanctioned by the GKO resolution of 22 September and 1 October 1942.

From the experience of many air battles, the following conclusions can be drawn:

- The Yak-7B could easily compete in aerial combat with the Me-109 in turns and verticals: in horizontal figures, the Yak-7B had an advantage and quickly entered the tail of the Me-109.

  The horizontal speeds of the Yak-7B and the Me-109 were approximately the same.

- The Yak-7B lagged behind the Me-109F in vertical figures.

  In a dive the Yak-7B fell behind, although for a very short time, so no full conclusions can be drawn.

The main disadvantages of the Yak-7B:

- It was heavy, which made it difficult to gain speed quickly.
- High resistance due to water and oil radiators.
- He didn't have a good rear view.
- The engine's power did not match the weight of the aircraft.
- When firing, you had to take your hand off the gas sector and move it to the trigger, which worsened control of the aircraft and also reduced aiming accuracy.

The Yak-7B with the upgraded M-105PF engine was a front-line fighter and differed from its predecessor, the Yak-7B with the M-105PA engine, primarily in the increased engine power from 1,050 to 1,180 hp.

Increased power at sea level and medium altitudes was achieved by modifying the setting of the P-7 automatic boost regulator, increasing boost pressure from 910 to 1,050 mm Hg.

- To ensure reliable operation in this "forced mode", the piston pins were strengthened and the carburetor settings were changed: otherwise, the M-105PF engine had no other design differences from the M-105PA.

The initiative to increase the thrust of the M-105PA engine belonged to the Design Bureau of A.S. Yakovlev, who in early 1942 on the Yak-7A N22-41 production aircraft conducted experiments to increase the engine's boost pressure successively to 950, 1,000 and 1,050 mm Hg.

The results of the experiments proved to be very encouraging and served as the basis for adopting a government decision obliging V. Ya. Klimov to convert the M-105PA engine from normal to forced operation as soon as possible.

In addition to the installation of a "forced engine", several measures were taken on the Yak-7B aircraft to improve aerodynamics and reduce the flying weight of the aircraft, mainly by improving and lightening the structural elements, without reducing drag and damaging the combat and operational qualities.

- The improved aerodynamics of the Yak-7B with the M-105PF engine gave it an advantage over the Me-109G-2 of 23 km/h at sea level and 16 km/h at an altitude of 1,000 meters.
- Conversely, at an altitude of 5,000 meters, the Me-109G-2 outperformed the Yak-7B M-105PF by 23 km/h, while above 5,000 meters the speed advantage of the Me-109G-2 became even more evident and reached 80 km/h.

In August 1941, on the instructions of the chief designer A.S. Yakovlev at plant number 301 on the basis of the Yak-7UTI, two prototypes were built in the version of the Yak-7R reconnaissance aircraft with the AFA-IM aerial cameras and the RSI-4 radio station.

The aircraft was metallized and shielded, slats, armored seatbacks and special glass were installed.

Armament consisted of a 20 mm ShVAK cannon with 120 rounds.

- These aircraft successfully passed state tests at the Research Institute of the Air Force Special Services in September 1941, but were not built in series due to the great demand for a single-seat Yak-7 fighter.

On the serial Yak-7B aircraft, seats with appropriate parts were provided for attaching the AFA-IM photographic installation.

Thus, additional equipment of aircraft for photo reconnaissance could be carried out by combat units directly in the field, in accordance with the technical documentation attached to the aircraft.

About 350 Yak-7B aircraft with photographic equipment for the AFA-IM camera were produced at plants No. 153 and No. 82.

Technique

Structurally unchanged from the Yak-1, the Yak-7 was also a low-wing monoplane whose fuselage was made of steel lattice with the front part covered in duralumin and the rear part covered in wood.

- The wings were wooden, with only the control surfaces made of fabric-covered duralumin.

The cockpit featured two seats in both the training versions and those intended to operate as a fighter aircraft: thanks to the second seat, the aircraft was also used for liaison flights or for small transports between departments.

Only in the "7B" version was the rear seat missing, replaced by an 80-litre fuel tank, also used as ballast, which was often removed by flight departments as it was not appreciated by pilots who feared its explosion during combat.

The fairing consisted of a long glass panel comprising three lateral elements; in the "7A" version the third glass element was replaced by a suitably shaped plywood panel.

- In the last examples produced in the "7B" version the canopy was of the "drop" type and the top of the fuselage was lowered, similarly to what was introduced on the Yak-1.

The landing gear was of the classic type and, in the design forecasts, was of the retractable type: this solution was used on all the examples of the fighter variants but was abandoned after a short period in the "7UTI" and "7V" training variants as the structural problems with the landing gear legs were considered dangerous and not suitable for a training aircraft.

In operational use, pilots were always advised against resorting to sudden use of the braking system, both to prevent the legs from collapsing and to prevent the nose from "sticking" during landing.

The oil and glycol radiators had been enlarged, to reduce overheating of the fluids, and angled slightly downwards.

The insulation of the structure was increased, the tail wheel became fully retractable: the joints and the cover were made more accurately, the propeller reduction gear worked better.

- An electro-pneumatic charging system was also installed, while the passenger compartment structure was reinforced.

Apart from a few experimental attempts, the Yak-7 was powered throughout its operational life by the Klimov M-105: this was a liquid-cooled V12 engine with a displacement of 35.1 L, the result of the development, supervised by Vladímir Âkovlevič Klímov, of the M-100 engine, a license-built copy of the Franco-Spanish Hispano-Suiza 12Y unit.

- The first version, M-105P, mounted on the Yak-7, Yak-7UTI and Yak-7V aircraft, was capable of developing about 1,050 hp (772 kW) of power.

The Yak-7As received the M-105PA variant which, while unchanged in power output, had modified crankcases and connecting rods, resulting in significant improvements in reliability.

- From the summer of 1942 the Yak-7Bs were equipped with the M-105PF version which gave the aircraft better performance, being able to deliver a power of 1,200 hp (883 kW).

The first Yak-7UTI training variant was equipped with two 7.62 mm ShKAS machine guns, while the Yak-7V variant was completely devoid of offensive armament.

In the case of the Yak-7 and Yak-7A fighters, the armament consisted of a 20 mm ShVAK cannon, firing through the propeller hub, and two 7.62 mm ShKAS machine guns, housed in the upper part of the nose, firing, by means of a synchronization system, through the propeller disk.

- In the Yak-7B models the two ShKAS were replaced with two 12.7 mm Berezin UBS.

Similar to the Yak-1, the Yak-7 could also be equipped with six RS-82 rocket projectiles: again, due to the deterioration of performance caused by aerodynamic effects, in the spring of 1942 the authorities issued orders calling for their decommissioning in favor of underwing loads consisting of free-fall bombs weighing up to a maximum of 200 kg.

- The Yak-7 was gradually replaced by the Yak-9, but until 1944 it enjoyed widespread and appreciable use , although little known as it remained in the shadow of the other Yaks.

At the end of the conflict, several Yak-7V trainers were supplied to the Polish Air Force and a single Yak-7V was delivered to the Hungarians with the task of familiarizing their pilots with the Yak-9 fighter.

Technical Features

Dimensions and weights

- Length: 8.47 meters
- Wingspan: 10.00 meters
- Height: 2.75 meters
- Wing area: 17.15 m ^{2}
- Empty weight: 2,480 kg
- Maximum take-off weight: 3,010 kg

Propulsion

- Engine: a Klimov VK-105PF 12-cylinder V
- Power: 1,260 hp

Performance

- Maximum speed: 610 km/h
- Autonomy: 825 km
- Tangency: 10,200 meters

Armament

- Machine guns: one Berezin UB caliber 12.7 mm or two ShKAS caliber 7.62 mm
- Guns: 1 x 20 mm ShVAK in the propeller hub
- Bombs: up to 200 kg
- Missiles: 6 RS-82 rockets.

Versions

- **UTI-26**

Originally designated as a two-seater trainer project, later designated Yak-7UTI.

- **Yak-7**

First variant developed from the original two-seater: cockpit of unchanged dimensions but single-seater, improved armament, retractable landing gear.

- **Yak-7A**

Second fighter variant: the radio was introduced, the semi-retractable tail wheel was reinstated, the canopy was modified, eliminating the rear glass part, replacing it with a wooden element, the instrument panel was modified and the oxygen system for the pilot was introduced.

- **Yak-7B**

This variant was fitted with an RSI-4 radio and introduced several aerodynamic improvements suggested by TsAGI; the two 7.62 mm ShKAS machine guns were replaced with two 12.7 mm Berezin UB machine guns.
At some point the M-105PF engine was installed to replace the earlier M-105PA.
Racks for carrying two bombs were also introduced, while those for the RS-82 rocket-propelled projectiles were removed.

- **Yak-7-37**

Version derived from the Yak-7B model, it provided for the use
of a 37 mm MPSh-37 cannon, firing through the propeller hub.
In August 1942, 22 examples were built and sent to the northern
part of the front for a series of operational trials which, having
been concluded positively, convinced the designers to continue
the development work of the cannon for installation on aircraft
of more recent design.

- **Yak-7M**

The acronym stood for a "modified" version.
One Yak-7UTI example was extensively modified: the single
ShKAS machine gun was replaced by three 20 mm ShVAK
cannons, one firing through the propeller hub and one arranged
in each wing half firing outside the propeller disc.
  - The wingspan was slightly reduced, and consequently the
    capacity of the tanks, which was remedied by placing an
    additional tank in the area of the second cockpit, behind
    the pilot, completely deprived of any equipment.

The wings were also marginally redesigned in their overall
shape and fitted with slats, improving the aircraft's stability and
reducing its stall speed.
These modifications, however, were not followed up in series
production as they would have required interventions that were
too radical compared to the standard.

- **Yak-7/M-82**

Prototype, dating back to the summer of 1941, equipped with a
Shvetsov M-82 engine, and intended to evaluate the opportunity
of creating a variant equipped with a radial engine.

The improved performance shown by the first prototypes of the Lavochkin La-5 with the same engine led to the abandonment of the experimentation.

• **Yak-7PD**

Prototype equipped with the M-105PD engine, featuring a new compressor and intended for use at high altitudes.
Built in the late summer of 1942, it was armed only with the 20 mm ShVAK cannon, but it did not deliver the expected performance, also due to the manual control of the compressor, and remained at the prototype stage.

• **Yak-7PVRD**

Designation given to two examples that mounted two Merkulov DM-4 ramjets under the wings: the aircraft were used for experimental flights aimed at studying the engines built by Igor Alekseevič Merkulov, also tested on the Bereznjak-Isaev BI prototype.

• **Yak-7R**

The acronym indicated its use as a reconnaissance aircraft: in chronological order it was one of the first modifications made to the original project.
Aircraft of this variant, armed with only the ShVAK cannon, were equipped with an AFA-I camera and RSI-4 radio.

• **Yak-7V**

Training variant developed in late 1944: the engine was the same as the Yak-1, a 1,260 hp Klimov M 105 PF.

- **Yak-7D and Yak-7DI**

Prototypes intended, respectively, to function as a reconnaissance aircraft and a long-range fighter: considerably modified in their original structure, they were put into production giving birth to the Yakovlev Yak-9.

Yakovlev Yak-9

The Yakovlev Yak-9 was a single-engine, low-wing fighter designed by OKB 115 under Alexander Sergeevich Yakovlev and developed in the Soviet Union in the 1940s.
Mainly used by the (VVS), it was used in war actions in the Second World War, starting from the second half of 1943 and by the North Korean Air Force, in the Korean War.

- Pilots who flew it considered its performance to be on par with the Messerschmitt Bf 109G and the Focke-Wulf Fw 190A-3/A-4, recently introduced on the Eastern Front.

It was the largest-built Soviet fighter in history.
16,769 were produced, 14,579 of which were during the war, and it remained in production from 1942 to 1948.
The main post-war operators, apart from the Soviet Union, were Bulgaria, Poland and Yugoslavia.
It was capable of outperforming the Messerschmitt Bf 109G in combat, with which it clashed in the skies over Stalingrad, and of facing the latest Focke-Wulf Fw 190 models on equal terms.

- It was also the first Soviet aircraft to score a victory against the Messerschmitt Me 262 jet aircraft.

The Yak-9 was originally a development of the 1941 Yak-7 fighter, of which 6,399 were built: it was from the Yak-7D, an experimental variant, that the new model was derived.

- The need to build a better series of these aircraft was dictated above all by the need to improve their autonomy.

The wing panels were partially redesigned, while the pilot's cockpit was moved slightly further back and the position of the radiator in the belly was also changed. Production began in the summer of 1942 and the Yak-9 was delivered to fighter units in October.

The aircraft's intense career, which began during the Battle of Stalingrad, did not prevent it from being upgraded, a process that initially concerned its armament.

Yak-9 used by the Normandie-Niemen Hunting Group.

In the Yak-9M version, the original 20 mm cannon and machine guns were supplemented by a 12.7 mm machine gun, while the load carrying capacity of the Yak-9B model was used to the maximum and the aircraft could carry a maximum bomb load of 400 kg (883 lb).

- This was followed by the Yak-9T, tested in December 1942 and operational from the beginning of the following year: it was designed for anti-tank use and was armed with the 37 mm Nudelmann-Suranov cannon.

In the summer of 1943, a new variant, the Yak-9D, entered service.

It had a more powerful engine and was intended for the role of a long-range escort fighter: in this aircraft the increase in range, which eventually exceeded 1,300 km (807 mi), was achieved by reducing the defensive armament to consist of a 20 mm cannon and a single 12.7 mm calibre machine gun.

A further improvement was made to the Yak-9DD, a version derived from it, in which the range was increased to 2,200 km (1,242 mi.

- These aircraft were used primarily to escort American bomber formations taking off from bases in Britain to carry out raids on oil fields in Romania.

The last variant to be built during the war was the Yak-9U, the prototype of which took flight in December 1943.

In this model, Yakovlev substantially renewed the airframe, redesigning its entire basic structure, which became completely metallic, like its skin, and significantly improving its aerodynamic lines.

- Furthermore, the wingspan and wing surface were increased, while a more powerful engine, the 1,650 hp Klimov M-107A, was adopted.

This greatly improved the aircraft's performance, increasing the maximum speed of 600 km/h (372 mph) at 3,500 metres (11,482 ft) achieved by the Yak-9D to around 700 km/h (434 mph) at 5,500 metres (18,092 ft).

It was from this aircraft that the final post-war version, the Yak-9P, was later developed.

The Yak-9 had 22 major modifications, 15 of which were mass-produced: it was equipped with five different types of new and modified engines, six variants of the number and volume of fuel tanks, seven variants of weapons and two variants of special equipment.

- It is worth noting that the Yak-9 had two significantly different types of wings: a mixed one and an all-metal one.

The Yak-9 was the most widely produced fighter aircraft by the Soviet Air Force during World War II: by mid-1944, the Yak-9, Yak-9T and Yak-9D aircraft outnumbered all other fighters in service and had largely replaced the Yak-1 and Yak-7B on the main fronts.

- The Yak-9 was mass-produced for six years, from October 1942 to December 1948. A total of 16,769 were built.

In addition to its long and intense career in VVS units, the Yakovlev Yak-9 also equipped numerous foreign units that chose to fight in the Soviet Union.

Among them were the Poles of the 1st Warsaw Fighter Regiment and the French of the Groupe de Chasse Normandie-Niernen, whose pilots chose the Yak-9 after trying the American Bell P-39 and the Hawker Hurricane.

After the war, apart from the Soviet Union, the Yak-9 was adopted mainly by Bulgaria, Poland and Yugoslavia.

History

The Yak-9 was the third major fighter type of the Yak family during World War II, after the Yak-1 and Yak-7.

From the design point of view, it was a further evolution of the Yak-7: although slightly different in appearance, the Yak-9 was at the same time more advanced in all respects.

The main innovation introduced in this prototype was the extensive use of duralumin, now available in quantity in the Soviet Union, which allowed a substantial reduction in the weight of the airframe and the consequent possibility of allocating the savings obtained to the use of greater quantities of equipment, armament and fuel.

- A particular advantage from the use of duralumin was obtained in the construction of the wing structure, in which the metal alloy replaced the wood of the spars and the six internal ribs, the two outermost ones being still made of wood.

Thanks to weight savings, self-sealing tanks with a total capacity of 833 litres of fuel were packed inside the wings, which gave the aircraft unmatched range values in the Yakovlev single-engine family.

- The structural innovation was combined with the creation of veneered plywood cladding impregnated with Bakelite in the wings.

The main feature of the Yak-9 was its ability to be modified into a wide range of aircraft types in terms of purpose and combat use, including a front-line fighter with conventional and heavy weapons, a long-range escort fighter, a fighter-bomber, a photo-reconnaissance fighter, a high-altitude fighter-interceptor, a two-seater unarmed special passenger aircraft, a two-seater trainer and transport fighter.

After the success of the Yak-1 project, Yakovlev's design bureau continued to work hard, also because the situation was still extremely critical: the Germans continued to inflict heavy losses on the Red Army along the entire front, while the VVS often failed to compensate, with courage and numbers, for the better combat technique of the Luftwaffe pilots.

- The Yak-7D prototype had been undergoing flight tests for just a few days when Yakovlev himself, on 16 June 1942, gave the order to transform the project into a long-range fighter aircraft.

In this case, the fuselage of a Yak-7B was used, but the rear part was modified by lowering it as on the Yak-7PD: the new light alloy wing was maintained but the maximum fuel capacity was reduced to 673 litres, while at the same time all the fuel system ducts were revised.

The aircraft in its new configuration was designated Yak-7DI and passed the trials at the NII-VVS in early August 1942 with excellent ratings.

- Its immediate serial production was therefore requested under the definitive name of Yak-9.

The Yak-9's armament was similar to that of the Yak-7DI: a 20 mm ShVAK motor cannon with 120 rounds and a 12.7 mm Berezin UBS synchronized machine gun (left) with 200 rounds.

The Yak-9 was highly maneuverable in both the vertical and horizontal planes, and was easy and pleasant to fly: it had a significant advantage in the air over other domestic and enemy fighters. For example, in a vertical combat, the Yak-9 would position itself on the tail of the Me-109F after the first combat turn, while in a horizontal combat - after 3-4 turns.

Production of the Yak-9 began in October 1942 and involved a total of three factories:

- No. 82, near Moscow, which built 817 aircraft between 1944 and 1945.
- Novosibirsk No. 153, which built a total of 12,536 aircraft from 1942 to 1948.
- No. 166 in Omsk, which built 3,416 examples from 1943 to 1945.

The Yak-9 M-106 was one of the first modifications of the serial Yak-9 M-105PF model: its creation was a response to the Battle of Stalingrad, which revealed the urgent need to improve aircraft performance.

As mentioned, the engines were completely interchangeable, so no modifications to the engine mounts, cowlings or other structural elements of the aircraft were necessary.

The Yak-9 M-106 aroused considerable interest in the Air Force: compared to the Yak-7 M-105PF it had a significant advantage in terms of maximum speed, rate of climb, maneuverability, especially at medium and high altitudes, practical ceiling and take-off properties, although in terms of piloting technique, it was practically no different from the Yak-1, Yak-7 and Yak-9 with the M-105PF engine.

- However, this aircraft was not built in series because the engine was not yet fully developed: the M-106 was therefore withdrawn from production in May 1943.

By December 1943, it was possible to install the more powerful M-107 engine on the airframe of a Yak-9U: the engine mount was new, the fuselage structures and wing spars were made of light alloy, the entire aircraft was covered with plywood, the engine had individual, shaped exhaust pipes.

The amount of fuel carried was increased to 402 litres (106 gallons).

- To recenter the model, the wing was repositioned ten centimetres forward and to "soften" the control column, the horizontal surfaces of the tail were slightly reduced.

The rear part of the cockpit was lengthened and the antenna cable was inserted inside the fuselage.

Armament retained the 20 mm ShVAK axial cannon, with 120 rounds and the pair of synchronized 12.7 mm Berezin UBS machine guns, with 170 rounds each.

State trials took place between January and April 1944 and revealed that the Yak-9U was a truly exceptional machine, with a marked superiority over every other fighter model operational at that time on the Eastern Front, at least up to 6,050 metres (19,800 ft).

- The aircraft's structure was strengthened and improved at every point, and the weapons and engines that could be fitted on board became the most varied the Soviets had ever managed to achieve with their single-seaters.

The aircraft was very easy to fly and very stable: unfortunately, it also manifested all the defects that afflicted the new M-107A engine, often the same ones that had already characterised the versions of the M-105 engine from which it was derived: overheating of the propulsion unit, oil leaks, decrease in pressure during climb, intense vibrations, rapid wear of the spark plugs and, above all, the short life of the engine, which did not exceed 25 hours.

Despite all these shortcomings, however, due to its outstanding performance, the Soviet authorities ordered the Yak 9U VK-107 to be put into production in April 1944.

- And by December 1944, 1,134 examples were produced.

Use

The first Yak-9s saw action in the Battle of Stalingrad in October 1942, immediately giving German fighters a hard time.

- Subsequently, Soviet fighters, often called the "Soviet Spitfires" due to their liquid-cooled engine design and excellent low-to-medium altitude performance, increasingly asserted themselves, achieving overall air superiority in the last two years of the war.

Their role also included anti-tank attack, tactical bombing, strategic and tactical escort for bombers.

In the last year of the war, the Yak-9U entered service, capable of outclassing any German fighter below 7,000 metres.

The Normandie-Niemen group, formed by French volunteers who fought on the Russian front, achieved 273 aerial victories with all types of Yakovlev fighters, but especially with the Yak-9 (according to some sources fewer, but still an impressive result for a single group that equalled the feats of the "Flying Tigers" in China).

- Both squadrons, with pilots of Polish nationality, also operated different versions of the first generation Yak-9.

Between 25 October and 25 December 1944, the 163.IAP was the first regiment to employ the Yak-9U in combat.

Pilots were ordered not to push the engine to "combat" speeds because this would reduce its lifespan to only two or three flights.

Despite this, during 398 sorties, the unit claimed 27 Focke-Wulf Fw 190As and one Bf 109G-2 shot down, compared to the loss of two Yaks in aerial combat, one shot down by flak, and four in accidents.

The Yak-9U played a major role in the Soviets' gaining air superiority, and the Germans soon learned to avoid engaging in combat with "mastless" Yaks.

A large formation of the 9DD version for very long escorts was transferred to Bari from Ukraine to assist the Yugoslav partisans.

The Yak-9 was also the first Soviet aircraft to score a victory against German Messerschmitt Me 262 jet aircraft: on 22 March 1945, LI Sivko of the 812.IAP shot down an Me 262 before being shot down and killed himself by another Messerschmitt jet pilot, probably Franz Schall, one of the German aces of the 262.

- In the post-war period, Yakovlev propeller-driven fighters were still very popular and saw combat in the Korean War, but were soon destroyed by US air action.

According to some sources, one of them even shot down a Boeing B-29 Superfortress bomber surprised at not very high altitude.

The model used was the "P", slightly improved compared to the wartime "U" model.

On May 8, 2007, in the French town of Les Andelys, in the memorial complex of the Normandy-Neman Division, a monument was unveiled, a Yakovlev Yak-9 aircraft dedicated to the French pilot Marcel Lefèvre.

The monument is installed near the entrance to the historical museum together with the Mirage F1 plane, which represents the present of the French Air Force.

Technique

The Yakovlev Yak-9 clearly showed its lineage from the Yak-1 and Yak-7 designs in its external lines.
The fuselage had a low rear section, already introduced in the Yak-1B and Yak-7B, with a drop-shaped cockpit.

- Both the nose shape, with the oil radiator positioned under the engine unit highlighted by the characteristic air intake, and that of the tail section were substantially unchanged.

The fuselage retained the steel lattice structure with the front part covered in duralumin and the rear part covered in wood.
The major element of discontinuity compared to previous aircraft was represented by the wing: for the first time, duralumin was used with which both the two spars and the first six of the eight ribs that made up the structure were made: the two ribs closest to the ends were, in fact, still made of wood.

- The wing covering also used a technique first used by the OKB-115: the wood used until then was replaced by plywood panels impregnated with Bakelite.

Two self-sealing fuel tanks were positioned inside the wings: unlike the two prototypes, the Yak-7D and Yak-7DI, the Yak-9 fighter carried a limited quantity of fuel, in order to maximise its handling and agility, made evident by the weight savings achieved thanks to the light alloy wing structure.
The landing gear was of the conventional type, with single-wheel main gear retracting into the wing towards the centre of the fuselage.

- The engine chosen to power the Yak-9 was the 12-cylinder Klimov M-105PF liquid-cooled V-engine, which had already been used on the Yak-7Bs for six months.

This engine was rated at 1,180 hp (880 kW) and gave the aircraft a maximum speed of 599 km/h at 4,300 metres altitude.

Lacking any drop armament, the Yak-9, in the fighter version, was armed with a 20 mm ShVAK cannon, firing through the propeller hub, and a 12.7 mm Berezin UBS machine gun housed above the engine in the left nose, and firing through the propeller disk by means of a synchronizing device.

The ammunition tanks held 120 and 200 shells respectively.

Technical Features

Dimensions and weights

- Length: 8.54 meters
- Wingspan: 9.80 meters
- Height: 2.44 meters
- Wing area: 17.23 m ^{2}
- Empty weight: 2,750 kg
- Maximum take-off weight: 3,200 kg
- Built: 14,240

Propulsion

- Engine: Klimov VK-105PF or Klimov VK-107A both 12-cylinder V-engine
- Power:
    - ❖ 1,260 hp Klimov VK-105 PF
    - ❖ 1,650 hp Klimov VK-107A

Performance

- Maximum speed: between 573 km/h (Yak-9D) and 700 km/h (Yak-9U)
- Autonomy: between 840 and 890 km
- Tangency: 10,500 meters

Armament

- Machine guns: two 12.7 mm BS
- Guns: 1 ShVAK 20 mm caliber

Versions

Yak-9 M-106

Prototype dating back to November 1942: single-seater fighter, in a configuration equivalent to that of the Yak-7DI.
Equipped with the Klimov M-106 engine with a single-speed mechanically controlled compressor: during acceptance trials it showed very similar performances, in terms of maximum speed and rate of climb, to those of the Yak-9 equipped with the M-105 engine.
The abandonment of the development of the engine unit caused the same fate as the corresponding Yak-1 M-106.

* **Yak-9**

First version, introduced in October and used in combat from the second half of December 1942, powered by a 1,180 hp Klimov M-105PF engine and equipped with a 12.7 mm Berezin UBS machine gun and a 20 mm ShVAK cannon.
459 examples were produced in factories Nos. 153 and 166 between October 1942 and August 1943.
A version powered by the 1,350 hp M-106 engine was also tested, a conversion that did not require any adaptation given the similarities between the two, but the performance was similar and it was not put into series production.

Yak-9B

The Yak-9B with VK-105PF engine was a modification of the serial Yak-9D N14-20 model.

Fighter-bomber version, it was equipped with four vertical bomb bays for a maximum load of 400 kg of bombs.

Also usable as a pure fighter, once the bombs were stowed on board the aircraft reached a weight of approximately 3,600 kg and its use in these conditions was reserved for expert pilots.

- It was characterized by the presence, behind the cockpit, of a bay for four 100 kg FAB-100 high explosive bombs or four "cluster bombs" each containing 32 PTAB submunitions weighing 2.5 kg each: in both cases the devices were arranged with the head up and inclined 15° towards the bow.

Yak-9B.

Production was limited to 109 examples delivered starting in the autumn of 1944: initially subject to flight accidents, caused largely by the poor quality of the workmanship, it also suffered from malfunctions of the PTAB ammunition which, in certain conditions, tended to explode upon release, causing serious damage to the aircraft itself.

Despite the positive results in combat use, the Yak-9B received, based on the results of military tests, an overall unsatisfactory assessment due to the lack of a special bomb sight, the difficulty of piloting with a bomb load of 500 and 400 kg and a full fuel tank, as well as the presence of such defects as the hovering of aerial bombs during dive bombing at an angle of 45-50°.

- Also considering the poor preparation of fighter pilots to face bombing missions, any further development was abandoned, despite the operational results obtained being encouraging.

In fact, 2,494 combat missions with bombing were carried out: 51,047 bombs were dropped for a total weight of 356.5 tons.

53 air battles were carried out, with 25 enemy aircraft shot down, including 20 FW-190s, 2 Me-109s, 1 Arado-56, two He-129s, against the loss of 8 Yak-9Bs in combat, of which 4 were shot down and 4 damaged.

Yak-9D

Single-seat, long-range fighter.

The Yak-9D with the M-105PF engine and VISh-61P propeller was a fighter with an increased flight range: in fact, it differed from the serial Yak-9 model mainly in fuel and lubricant reserves.

Instead of two 440-liter fuel tanks, four tanks were installed for a total of 650 liters, while the lubrication system increased to 48 kg instead of the 25 kg of the Yak-9.

- The fuel tank capacity was distributed as follows: two tanks of 208 litres each and two tanks of 117 litres each.

A three-way fuel valve was installed in the cabin, which allowed the engine to be refueled separately from the right or left tank groups, or from both tank groups simultaneously.

Yak-9D.

Developed by exaggerating the concept of long range, which had already led to the birth of the Yak-9 model, this version was created by OKB-115 through further strengthening of the wing structure, in particular the ribs, inside which were created the four metal tanks capable of containing a total of, as mentioned, 650 litres of fuel.

- The variant went into production from May 1944 and a total of 399 examples were built.

To limit, at least in part, the increase in overall weight, the armament was reduced to the 20 mm ShVAK cannon with 120 rounds, and a single 12.7 mm Berezin UBS synchronized machine gun with 200 rounds (left).

- A serious disadvantage of the early production Yak-9D as an escort fighter was the lack of an artificial horizon and a radio compass, which limited its use in adverse weather conditions.

Thus, subsequently, particular attention was dedicated to radio communication equipment, with the installation of SCR-274N equipment of American origin, and to radio navigation equipment, equipping the aircraft with an RPK-10 radio direction finder.

Despite the increase in weight, and the consequent deterioration in its handling characteristics, the aircraft remained capable of operating from unprepared surfaces and, thanks to its declared range of 905 km, was used both for escort operations for bombing units and to counter enemy aircraft beyond the front line.

Experience in air combat showed that the Yak-9D had an advantage over the Me-109G-2 and FW-190A-8 in turns up to an altitude of 3,500 meters, and, when about half of its fuel supply was exhausted, it also had an advantage in vertical maneuvers.

- **Yak-9M**

Single-seat long-range fighter.
It was essentially an update of the "9D" variant using the "9T" fuselage in which the different weight distribution, due to the

relocation of the cabin, had proved advantageous from the point of view of the fighter's maneuverability and agility.

The choice also allowed for standardization of production, being able to complete only one type of cell without any more distinctions between the two variants.

- Production, which began in May 1944, totaled 4,239 units.

Some of these were completed to the standard defined as Yak-9M/PVO: intended for the Vojska PVO they were equipped with night search lights and all-weather radio navigation equipment.

From October 1944 all completed aircraft were equipped with the 1,240 hp (925 kW) VK-105PF2 engine.

Yak-9DD

The Yak-9DD was a fighter with an even greater fuel capacity, and was a modification of the serial Yak-9D and Yak-9T models with the VK-105PF engine.
The modification was made by the design bureau in connection with the need, which emerged in 1944, to have a fighter with an even greater flight range than the Yak-9D, capable of performing the task of escorting bombers during their operations in the enemy's rear.

- Eight fuel tanks with a total capacity of 845 litres were installed, all made of metal, with protection against bullets up to 7.62 mm calibre (protection thickness equal to 15 mm), while the capacity of the oil tank was increased to 70 litres.

As armament it had only the 20 mm ShVAK cannon with 120 rounds, but it was equipped with special equipment for night flights and in adverse weather conditions: SCR-274N radio station with two BC-454A and BC-455A receivers and two BC-457A and BC-459A transmitters, RPK-10M radio compass, AG-2 artificial horizon, higher main antenna and additional antenna, more powerful generator and battery, 8-liter oxygen cylinder instead of 4-liter.

- The flying weight of the Yak-9DD was thus increased by 270 kg over the Yak-9D and by 362 kg over the Yak-9T, settling at 3,387 kg.

Due to the increased weight, the flight and tactical data at full load changed significantly: the maximum speed decreased, the rate of climb, maneuverability and take-off and landing properties worsened, but, after using half of the fuel reserve, the maximum speed and other data became practically the same as those of the serial Yak-9D model.

Yak-9DD during their mission in Italy.

Thanks to the significant increase in fuel reserves, by more than 30% compared to the Yak-9D, the range and flight duration were significantly increased: in fact, the flight range before complete fuel exhaustion was increased to 1,325 km.
The Yak-9DD was mass-produced from May 1944 to September 1945. 399 were built.

Yak-9K

Single-seater fighter, with a VK-105PF engine and a VISh-61P propeller with a diameter of 3.0 meters, it was equipped with a Nudelman-Suranov NS-45 cannon, with a belt of 29 shells, and a 20 mm Berezin UBS machine gun with 200 rounds.

From the construction point of view, it was a modification of the production Yak-9T aircraft, from which it differed mainly in that instead of the 37 mm NS-37 cannon, a 45 mm NS-45 cannon was installed.

A total of 53 examples were built, delivered between April and July 1944.

The NS-45 gun generated 40% more recoil than the NS-37 so it was fitted with a muzzle brake that could absorb most of it.

Yak-9K. Note the muzzle brake protruding from the propeller nose cone.

To reduce recoil, the barrel was equipped with a powerful muzzle brake, which absorbed up to 85% of the gun's recoil energy: the muzzle brake protruded 370 mm from the propeller nose cone, so the overall length of the Yak-9K was 8.87 m , compared to 8.66 m for the Yak-9T and 8.50 m for the Yak-9.

- The cannon and machine gun could be operated separately or simultaneously by two electric buttons on the aircraft's control stick.

The higher the flight speed and dive angle, the less impact the recoil had on the aircraft: aimed fire was possible and effective at speeds above 350 km/h and with short bursts of 2-3 shots.

- However, the aircraft structure was subjected to significant shaking that put a strain on the aircraft structure, also causing leaks of coolants and lubricants from the seals of their respective systems.

These critical elements, combined with the insufficient reliability of the cannon, were the main cause of the limited production of the version: externally, the aircraft of this version were easily recognizable by the cannon barrel which protruded well beyond the end of the propeller nose cone.

Due to the increased flying weight, the maximum speed of the Yak-9K, compared to the Yak-9T, was decreased by 32 km/h at an altitude of 5,000 meters, while the time to climb to 5,000 meters was increased to 6.5 minutes.

Yak-9P

Prototype, built in March 1943.

It was a standard Yak-9 in which the Berezin UBS machine gun had been replaced by a second ShVAK cannon, equipped with a reserve of 175 shells: it was tested in the second half of April but no series production was ordered.

It reached 670 km/h and had an initial climb rate of 1,500 metres per minute.

- **Yak-9P VK-107A**

Single-seater fighter.

The designation "9P", already used for a prototype in March 1943, was revived after the war to identify a new version of the Yak-9, which would also be the last one built.

- It was an aircraft with an all-metal structure requested by the authorities in June 1946.

The first two prototypes were flown in early summer: their armament was based on a central cannon, as mentioned, the type could be varied with ease, and two in the upper part of the nose.

- Some experimental examples were built, 20 of which had only the wing structure made of metal and 10 with the use of duralumin also in the rear part of the fuselage.

Series production was oriented towards the model made entirely of metal and reached a total of 772 units, completed at the end of March 1948.

Exported to several countries, these aircraft were the last Yak-9s to remain operational and were identified by the NATO reporting name "Frank".
Some examples were purchased by the North Korean Air Force and used during the Korean War.

Yak-9R

Photographic reconnaissance aircraft, single-seater.
Variant built from both Yak-9 and Yak-9D airframes.
A total of 35 aircraft were completed, equipped with cameras arranged perpendicular to the direction of flight.
In some cases, the "9D" aircraft had the nose machine gun removed to reduce overall weight.

- **Yak-9S**

Prototype dating back to spring 1945.
- It was one of the last attempts to improve the basic model equipped with the M-105 engine.

It used a new, more efficient propeller, but the most impactful change was in its armament, which was based on a Nudelman-Suranov NS-23 cannon, firing through the propeller hub, and two new 20 mm Berezin B-20 cannon, arranged in the upper part of the nose and synchronized with the movement of the propeller.
Two examples were built and subjected to evaluation tests in the summer of 1945 but, since the aircraft's characteristics proved to be inferior to those of the Yak-3 and the Lavochkin La-7, it was decided not to start series production.

Yak-9T

Single-seater fighter, 2,748 examples produced.
Armed with a Nudelman-Suranov NS-37 cannon, caliber 37 mm with 32 shells, firing from the propeller hub replacing the ShVAK, it retained the 12.7 mm Berezin UBS machine gun and the M-105PF engine.

Yak-9T prototype.

To accommodate the large-caliber gun, the fuselage was extended by 15 cm and structurally strengthened, while the cockpit was moved back by 40 cm.

- Weighing about 175 kg more than the Yak-9, it also had only two fuel tanks and, consequently, its range was reduced from 660 to 620 km.

Given the number of available projectiles, the aiming procedures had to be particularly accurate and, also due to the force of the recoil, the pilot could not fire more than three projectiles at a time.

The armament proved devastating against aircraft and also allowed successes against tanks and surface ships.

- **Yak-9TK**

Prototype, flown in October 1943.

It was used to experiment with the possibility of mounting different types of cannon, depending on the specific request from the VVS, simply by varying the attachments and the tanks with the ammunition.

- Alternatively, the 20 mm ShVAK, the 23 mm Volkov-Yartsev VYa-23, the 37 mm NS-37 or the 45 mm Nudelman-Suranov NS-45 could be used.

The solution did not find immediate application in series production, but was developed later in time with more modern weapons.

Yak-9U

Single-seater fighter.

The decision to proceed with a new step in the development of the Yak-9 dates back to the last months of 1943: following the indications provided by the TsAGI on the subject of aerodynamics, the Yak-9M was significantly modified, in particular, in its external shape, with the abandonment of the large oil radiator placed centrally under the nose, replaced by two circular radiators placed under the cockpit, towards which the air was conveyed through two air intakes obtained at the root of the leading edge of the wings, and in the fuselage covering, which saw the use of plywood panels instead of the fabric used until then.

- It had the 1,650 hp Klimov VK-107A engine and in early 1943 the prototype reached 700 lb/h (435 mph), which was remarkable for the time.

In this configuration the Yak-9 was almost unrecognisable from the Yak-3, except for its larger wingspan and the landing gear bay enclosure panels.

- The planned armament consisted of a 23 mm Volkov-Yartsev VYa-23 cannon, firing from the propeller hub, and two synchronized 20 mm Berezin UBS machine guns in the nose.

Tested between the end of 1943 and the first days of 1944, the new prototype showed remarkable performances, but was not admitted to series production, because the VYa-23 cannon was considered ineffective: furthermore, the aim was to use the more powerful VK-107 engine to obtain even better performances.

The first attempt to install the VK-107 on a Yak-9 dated back to February 1943 but an engine failure caused a flight accident with subsequent delays to the program: new attempts were made by equipping a limited number of Yak-9s, including eight of the "9D" version, with the new engine, whose problems, however, were still far from being solved.

Test flights resumed with a new prototype designated Yak-9U VK-107A, which was taken into flight on the same days in December 1943 as its "twin" powered by the M-105PF2.

Yak-9U.

In this case, however, the ShVAK cannon was chosen, as it was considered more reliable.

- Subsequent acceptance tests with state authorities showed very impressive performances, with the aircraft reaching a speed of 700 km/h at 5,500 metres, but it was once again confirmed that the engine problems would not have been manageable in the workshops of the front-line departments.

The aircraft was, however, put into production, as the authorities expected that the problems of overheating and leakage of lubricating oil would soon be solved.

From April 1944 the Yak-9U was produced at all three factories that had already produced the previous models and, despite continuing difficulties, the "9U" was in large-scale use by late summer 1944 with satisfactory operational results.

A total of approximately 2,500 were produced, of which approximately 750 were in service at the end of the war.

- **Yak-9UT**

Single-seater fighter.

Version derived from the "9U", starting from a prototype modified with the installation of a large-caliber cannon on whose model, however, the sources do not agree: in fact, there are indications regarding the use of the aforementioned NS-37 and NS-45, or of a weapon identified as "Nyukhtikov N-37".

In any case, after the tests were completed in March 1945, the aircraft was put into production equipped with a single NS-23 cannon firing from the propeller hub and two Berezin B-20s in the upper nose. A total of 282 aircraft were produced.

Yak-9UV

Prototype for a new training version, flown in June 1945.

It essentially combined the two-seater structure of the "9V" with that of the "9U", while the planned armament was limited to a single Berezin B-20 cannon installed between the engine banks.

Acceptance tests of the aircraft were carried out starting in July, but it was now clear that we were moving towards the jet age and operational needs required a completely new aircraft, so series production was not started.

- **Yak-9V**

Two-seater training aircraft.

From a design point of view, it was a modification of the standard Yak-9T, which was derived from the Yak-9M, and differed in that it had two cockpits located one behind the other, one for the student, at the front, and one for the instructor, at the rear, covered by a common canopy.

It had an armament based only on the 20 mm ShVAK cannon with 90 rounds, while paying particular attention to the on-board instrumentation, intended for both the instructor and the pilot, both for navigation and communications.

- A total of 793 aircraft were produced: 456 new ones rolled off the assembly lines of GAZ No. 153, while another 337 were built by converting Yak-9Ms.

The Yak-9V was practically no different from the Yak-9T, which was a great advantage for this aircraft: in terms of piloting technique and ease of landing, the Yak-9V was slightly inferior due to insufficient longitudinal stability due to the rearward shift of the center of gravity. And performing aerobatics and landings became more difficult, but not significantly.

- **Yak-9 Courier**

Prototype, built on the basis of the Yak-9V with the wing of the Yak-9DD.
Intended for liaison roles, particularly for carrying a passenger over long distances and in areas dangerously close to combat areas.
The passenger compartment was equipped with comfortable seats and each of the two occupants also had access to a urinal.
The aircraft was not even subjected to evaluation tests and there is no information regarding its actual use.

Yakovlev Yak-15

The Yakovlev Yak-15 was a single-engine, straight-wing jet fighter aircraft designed by OKB 115 under Alexander Sergeevich Yakovlev and developed in the Soviet Union in the late 1940s.

Used in the following years by the VVS, it remained operational from 1947 to the early 1950s until its progressive replacement with the subsequent Yak-17.

- Derived from the earlier propeller-driven Yak-3, the Yak-15 was the first jet fighter built in the Soviet Union.

It was one of the few fighters, including the Saab 21R, to be a conversion of a successful piston-engined model, but it was less successful than its later counterpart, the MiG-9: the I-300 prototype, presented on the same day, was flown two hours earlier, based on the outcome of a coin toss.

History

On April 9, 1945, the Council of People's Commissars contacted OKB Yakovlev requesting the development of a new single-seat jet fighter that would be equipped with the Junkers Jumo 004 turbojet acquired during the Soviet counteroffensive in the late stages of World War II.

In order to speed up its construction, Yakovlev based the design of the new model, designated as the Yak-3-Jumo, on the latest version of his Yakovlev Yak-3, a successful fighter equipped with a 12-cylinder V-engine.

To this end, the Klimov M-105 was removed from the Yak-3 airframe and the Jumo 004 jet engine was mounted under the front part of the fuselage, so that the exhaust gases exited from the central part of the underside of the fuselage, protected by a steel plate that preserved it from damage caused by the heat of the jet, giving the model a "pod-and-boom" configuration.

- Modifications to the original fuselage, already made of metal, were limited, except for the nose of the aircraft.

This was redesigned to accommodate, in the upper part, the armament based on a pair of 23 mm Nudelman-Suranov NS-23 aircraft cannons, an additional fuel tank above the engine and the engine itself.

No changes were made to the wing panels other than the removal of the oil cooling intakes and the bending of the stringer into an inverted U-shape to clear the engine.

- The empennage was modified only in the fin, which was slightly enlarged, while the horizontal planes remained unchanged.

The landing gear remained unchanged, a conventional rear tricycle retractable in its main elements, except for the tailwheel, adopting a leaf spring device to absorb ground irregularities.

- In total, the Yak-Jumo's available fuel load reached 590 kg.

Taxiing tests, which began in April 1945, revealed the first problems: the thermal protection proved too short-lived as the heat from the engine exhaust managed to melt the duralumin skin of the rear part of the fuselage, as well as melting the rubber of the tire in the tailwheel.

At the end of December, a first modification program was launched to correct the problems encountered.

In the meantime, a second prototype was completed, featuring an all-steel tail wheel and larger-span horizontal empennage elements.

After some taxiing tests it was transferred to TsAGI for full-scale wind tunnel testing, which lasted until May. On the 26th of the same month, the Council of People's Commissars released specifications for the aircraft, which was to reach a maximum speed of 770 km/h at sea level and 850 km/h at 5,000 metres (16,400 ft).

It would also have had to be able to climb to that altitude in at least 4 minutes and 30 seconds, and have a range of 500 km at 90% of maximum speed.

- Two prototypes were to be ready for flight tests by September 1.

According to aviation historians Bill Gunston and Yefim Gordon, on May 5, 1945, representatives of OKB 115 (Yakovlev) and 155 (MiG) tossed a coin to decide which would be the first Soviet jet aircraft to take flight: the Yak-Yumo or the competing I-300, the prototype of the future MiG-9.

At that juncture Yakovlev lost and the Yak-Jumo circled the airfield two hours later than the I-300.

The flight test phase was concluded on 22 June, however, early successes in the field of jet aviation resulted in a new specification, issued by the Sovmin (Council of Ministers of the Soviet Union) on 29 April, for two prototypes powered by the Soviet-built Tumanskij RD-10 engine (designated as Yak-15, Yak-15RD10 or Yak-RD).

Apart from the new engine, the requirements differed from the previous one only in the range, brought to 700 km at the optimum cruising speed, and in the reduction of the maximum ceiling to 14,000 metres (45,930 ft).

The two prototypes were to be ready for flight tests by 1 September 1946.

Yakovlev easily managed to adapt the airframes of the two existing prototypes to the RD-10s and one of the two was able to participate in the Tushino air parade in August 1946.

The day after the air demonstration, Stalin summoned Artyom Mikoyan and Alexander Yakovlev to his office and ordered that their OKBs should build 15 aircraft to take part in the November 7 parade on Red Square to commemorate the 30th anniversary of the October Revolution.

- For the construction of the new aircraft, the State Plant No. 31 in Tbilisi was chosen, which had already been the production line of the conventional Yak-3, and which would, therefore, be easily converted to the production of the new jet fighter.

All 15 examples were built ahead of schedule and, although not yet fully equipped and with incomplete avionics, were fitted with an enlarged fuel tank in place of the armament: following the cancellation of the parade, two examples were modified to adopt a single 23 mm cannon, which began the government acceptance testing programme which lasted until April 1947.

- The tests revealed a series of problems, both design-related, which in that configuration prevented an improvement in the model, and related to operational use.

The thick-profile wing inherited from the Yak-3 limited the maximum speed achievable, furthermore the positioning of the engine nozzle, due to the flow of hot air exiting downwards during taxiing, damaged the runway surface.

The pilots' conditions were also put to the test, as kerosene and lubricating oil frequently dripped onto the engine, causing smoke to enter the cockpit, and the model's range was also rather limited.

- All this aside, the Yak-15 was considered by test pilots to be very easy to fly, even by those who had only flown piston-engine fighters.

The latter aspect prevailed and, in the end, the VVS decided to accept the model in the role of advanced trainer aircraft with the task of training pilots who were destined for future jet fighters.

Even before the tests had been completed, the Council of Ministers ordered the start of production in December 1946, with an initial supply batch of 50 examples, to be built between January and April 1947, equally divided between single-seater aircraft and two-seater trainers, and armed with a single cannon. At that stage the two-seater training version encountered serious development difficulties, so that all the examples built belonging to the first batch were single-seaters.

- Final production, which concluded before the end of that year, amounted to 280 Yak-15s excluding prototypes.

The first example of the first production batch built by Plant No. 31, in the autumn of 1946, was a prototype of a two-seater trainer version, which remained the only one built in that configuration.

The prototype featured a redesigned fuselage to house a second cockpit at the front for the student pilot, which was accessed from a common canopy hinged on one side, and from which the armament was accessible.

Although the differences from the single-seaters were limited, its development was delayed and flight tests did not begin until 5 April 1947.

The only known surviving Yak-15 is "Yellow 37", which is on display at the Vadim Zadorozhniy Technical Museum in Moscow Oblast.